# THE
# *Mediterranean House*
# IN AMERICA

**LAUREN WEISS BRICKER**

*Photography by* **JUERGEN NOGAI**

# THE Mediterranean House IN AMERICA

ABRAMS, NEW YORK

# CONTENTS

# INTRODUCTION

## *The Appeal*
## *of the Mediterranean*

*Here is our Mediterranean! Here is our Italy! It is a Mediterranean without marshes and without malaria, and it does not at all resemble the Mexican Gulf. . . . It is a Mediterranean with a more equable climate, warmer winters and cooler summers, than the North Mediterranean shore can offer; it is an Italy whose mountains and valleys give almost every variety of elevation and temperature.*

CHARLES DUDLEY WARNER
*Our Italy* (1891)

AT THE TURN OF THE TWENTIETH CENTURY, THE AMERICAN WEST AND
Southeast were seen as Edens, abundantly fertile, sparsely populated regions of great, untapped promise. Journalist
Charles Dudley Warner exulted over Southern California's riches in his book, *Our Italy*, after a visit in 1890. Real estate
promoters enticed migrants from the Northeast and Midwest to California and Florida by extolling the potential of
agricultural development in "our commercial Mediterranean."[1] A wide range of produce could be cultivated in California, while in Florida the orange was king.[2] In their advertisements, railroads, acting as, or in partnership with, land
speculators, drew parallels between the climate and landscape of the Mediterranean and those of the Southwest, Texas,
California, and Florida to attract tourists and permanent residents.[3] Underscoring and building on those parallels, real
estate developers turned to Mediterranean sources for their architectural inspiration, in the process creating a new cultural landscape.[4]

By the mid-1920s the Mediterranean house in America represented an amalgamation of elements derived from
the domestic architecture of Spain, Italy, North Africa, and the Spanish colonies of the New World. Architects
sought not to re-create a specific house or even type of house found abroad, but to capture its character and mood and
translate it into terms that would be comfortable to an American audience. Typical features were white stucco walls,
red tile roofs, and an emphasis on outdoor spaces, including central courtyards, terraces, and loggias. In contrast
to the rectilinear symmetry of the popular center-hall Colonial, the houses were characteristically laid out in L- or
U-shaped courtyard plan or arranged in a rambling form so that the main rooms had access to the outdoors. Ironwork,

carved woodwork, decorative tiles, and fountains were common ornaments. Architect and writer Rexford Newcomb described the Mediterranean Revival style this way:

> Spanish, Italian, Moorish, Byzantine—Mediterranean types generally—instead of being kept archaeologically segregated, are under this orchestral process merged, as were those golden threads of long ago, into a new sun-loving style which, while eminently American in its plan and utilities, is never-the-less distinctly Mediterranean in its origins and spirit.[5]

European precedents for America's Mediterranean houses were the products of centuries of adaptation to climatic conditions, and, Newcomb argued, their tested success made them suitable to similar conditions in America in the days before central heating and air conditioning. They offered valuable lessons on planning and siting that integrated cross ventilation and solar orientation; insulating against extreme temperature fluctuations with thick masonry walls sheathed with concrete plaster (or, where wood-frame construction was prevalent, double-wall construction); and the cooling properties of terra-cotta roof and floor tiles. The houses of arid North Africa, with flat roofs that served as patios in the cool of the evening and drought-tolerant gardens, offered solutions for the Southwest; similarly, the houses built along Venice's canals presented useful models for humid Florida, such as window placement that maximized the circulation of air.

Americans were exposed to the Mediterranean style on grand tours abroad in the late nineteenth and early twentieth centuries. They sought to replicate the great houses and gardens of England, France, and Italy both to represent their own wealth (which was quickly accumulating in the years prior to federal income tax) in an analogous manner[6] and to imbue their new homes with the patina of age. Another kind of appropriation could be seen in California, the Southwest, Texas, and Florida, where houses were often modeled after the rural Italian villa or the Spanish farmhouse, lending timeless pastoral appeal to brand-new suburban developments or country estates.[7]

The Mediterranean style became a staple of American suburbs from coast to coast in the years between the two world wars and remains widely popular to this day. It is by far the prevailing house type in California, parts of the Southwest, Texas, and Florida, where thousands of Mediterranean Revival homes were built between the wars and where the style continues to dominate new construction. Even in the Northeast, where parallels to the mild Mediterranean are tenuous and Colonials and Tudors are more common, every affluent suburb includes a sampling of Mediterranean houses to round out its architectural diversity. Interpretations of the style have evolved over the past century from traditional to modern and back again, but the simplicity and embrace of the outdoors that remain at its core have proven the Mediterranean house to be both highly adaptable to changing tastes and enduringly attractive.

## Leading with the Landscape

The Mediterranean house in America could be said to have sprung from the garden. For many houses in southern Europe, where the emphasis is on outdoor living, the landscape is the dominant design element; the house itself often serves as an almost neutral passage to the courtyard or garden. Even before the Mediterranean Revival became an architectural trend, Americans nationwide began installing elaborately designed Italian- and Spanish-style gardens on the grounds of their distinctly non-Mediterranean houses.

Americans' interest in adapting Italian gardens to their own soil was stimulated by the book *Italian Gardens* (1894), by Charles A. Platt, a landscape painter who turned to garden design and then to architecture. Platt presented important examples of Italian gardens from the Renaissance and Baroque periods to demonstrate ways of designing landscape and architecture as an integrated composition. Italian villas typically were oriented to take advantage of views into landscape, and the adjacent gardens were organized into formal, geometric shapes, reiterating the house's footprint. The gardens became less structured as they receded from the house, until they merged with the distant view. Platt's publication was soon followed by other influential American works on the subject, such as Edith Wharton's *Italian Villas and Their Gardens* (1904) and Guy Lowell's *Smaller Italian Villas and Farmhouses* (1916).

One of the properties featured in *Italian Villas* was the Villa Gamberaia (fig. 1), whose garden Wharton called "probably the most perfect example of the art of producing a great effect on a small scale."[8] It exemplifies the Mediterranean approach to designing the outdoors into distinct living spaces.

*Fig. 2*    Charles A. Platt. Weld (Larz Anderson estate), Brookline, Massachusetts. 1901. Courtesy of Historic New England, Boston

*The garden is but the prolongation of the house, and as a house containing a single huge room would be less interesting and less serviceable than one divided according to the varied requirements of its inmates, so a garden which is merely one huge outdoor room is also less interesting and less serviceable than one which has its logical divisions.*[9]

The villa itself, which was built in 1610 in Settignano, outside Florence, has an architectural simplicity, unencumbered by surface ornament, that gives it an ageless quality. Four hundred years after its construction, it became a popular model for American houses (see La Toscana and Villa Calafia).

Platt himself translated the architectonic features of Italian gardens into landscapes he designed for his family, friends, and eventually clients (fig. 2).[10] In doing so, Platt broke from the prevailing picturesque school of American landscape architecture, led by Frederick Law Olmsted, who had gained national stature with his "natural garden" design for New York City's Central Park (1857–59). By advocating instead for classical design principles, Platt led a new landscape movement — one that accorded with the contemporary Beaux Arts movement in architecture. Young American architects were going to Paris to study at the École des Beaux-Arts, and American schools of architecture were patterning their curricula on the École's,[11] leading to the restrained, symmetrical, classically inspired designs of many buildings constructed between 1885 and 1920.

As with Italian-style landscape, the attraction of the Spanish garden preceded the fashion for the Spanish house in America. Owing to

extensive publications, Americans were most familiar with the gardens of Andalusia or southern Spain, a region that had been under Islamic control from 711 to about 1300. The gardens of Granada's Alhambra palace and the adjacent Generalife villa, and of the Alcazar castle in Seville, were included in illustrated travel guides, and beginning in the 1910s numerous books were published on the architecture, gardens, and decorative arts of Spain.[12] Paintings of the gardens captured the shimmering light and movement of plants, with details of the architecture subordinated to the atmospheric effects (fig. 3).[13]

In contrast with the rigorous geometry of Italian gardens, the appeal of Spanish landscape was rooted in its romance and exoticism.[14] It was inspired by the courtyard gardens of the arid Middle East, which were well suited to Andalusia, where water was equally scarce. The gardens are organized into discrete spaces that function as outdoor rooms. Water, introduced sparingly at centrally positioned fountains, drains through narrow troughs lined with colorful tile, helping to cool the gardens and adding an audible dimension. Beds of flowering plants are bordered by clipped hedges, and tall cypress, palm, and citrus trees provide shade and visually link the spaces. A covered walkway or corridor connects the garden to the house. Another surface treatment is

*Fig. 3*    Joaquín Sorolla y Bastida. *Corner of the Garden, Alcazar, Sevilla.* Oil on canvas, 37 x 25" (95.3 x 63.5 cm). 1910. J. Paul Getty Museum, Los Angeles

the paved patio, with plantings around the perimeter and in pots. By the mid-1920s similar features had been widely adopted in America, where Spanish-style gardens enjoyed great popularity.[15]

## Origins of the Style

The courtyard-plan house—a one- or two-story masonry house that was oriented inward, around an open-air core—was a Greco-Roman tradition found throughout the Mediterranean. The Romans, borrowing the courtyard plan from the Greeks and earlier Mesopotamian civilizations, developed villas in urban, suburban, and rural variants that in turn inspired houses across southern Europe, with design modifications during the fifteenth through seventeenth centuries. The best-known Italian variants are the *villa rustica*, which included outbuildings associated with agricultural production (workers' housing, stables, pens); the *villa suburbana*, designed as a retreat from the city, with landscape, usually terraced,[16] the dominant feature; and the *villa urbana*, also set out in nature but more spatially contained.[17] The *villa suburbana* was the most popular model for American house design. However, on larger properties with multiple buildings, the main house might reference the *villa suburbana*, while the configuration and arrangement of secondary buildings might recall the *villa rustica* (see Villa Calafia).

American houses based on the *villa urbana* incorporated at least one of three features found to be typical of the ancient Roman city house during archaeological investigations of Pompeii: an atrium near the entrance; a peristyle or colonnaded courtyard, usually at the center of the floor plan; and exterior walls that open to a garden at the rear of the property.[18] Such houses are often referred to as Pompeiian houses, though this type was not exclusive to Pompeii. Frescoes depicting garden scenes or the illusion of views out to gardens decorated the solid interior walls of many houses in Pompeii. American variants incorporate color into the wall surface—on its interior, exterior, or occasionally both (see Andrew Lawson House).

The leading Spanish precedent for Mediterranean houses in America was the Andalusian farmhouse, a humble dwelling built throughout southern Spain's countryside and small towns. It was composed of simple cubic volumes, one or two stories in height, that enclose modest courtyards (fig. 4). Whitewashed masonry walls with shed roofs covered in terra-cotta tile were left blank, except for the unadorned

*Fig. 4*  Austin Whittlesey. Drawing of Andalusian farmhouse. From *The Minor Ecclesiastical, Domestic, and Garden Architecture of Southern Spain* (New York: Architectural Book Publishing Co., 1917)

front door and the occasional small windows, placed asymmetrically in response to interior requirements.

An alternative to the farmhouse's bare exterior was the elaborate Churrigueresque door surround, which derived from seventeenth- and eighteenth-century ecclesiastical sources. The high relief contrasted dramatically with the simplicity of the rest of the house. In America, Churrigueresque detailing came into use following the 1915 Panama-California Exposition, held in San Diego. Bertram Grosvenor Goodhue, architect of many of the exposition's buildings, applied ornament derived from the Mexican adaptation of the Churrigueresque to his work there, most notably at the California Building (now the Museum of Man).[19]

The rustic courtyard of the Andalusian farmhouse—with cobblestone paving and exposed staircases leading to a cantilevered balcony—would occasionally be included in the design of Spanish houses in America. Often, however, the courtyards of these farmhouses were inspired by those of more formal houses or Moorish palaces, such as the Alhambra and the Alcazar, whose courtyards or patio gardens could be extremely ornate. Covered walkways encircled the courtyard, suggesting a cloister. A second story was often located above them, and colonnades or arcades (or a combination) of wood or masonry would support the overhang. Glazed ceramic tiles—an Islamic decorative tradition the Moors introduced to Spain—elaborated the dados (lower walls) of the courtyard and highlighted other architectural features throughout the house. The fashion for tile carried over to the Spanish colonies in Cuba and Mexico, which eventually developed their own tile works and later became important sources of glazed tile for Spanish-style houses in America.

## The Emergence of the Mediterranean in America

A taste for Mediterranean-inspired architecture in the United States was stimulated by the late nineteenth-century Mission Revival, which deconsecrated the ecclesiastical architecture of the Franciscan missions of North America's Spanish colonies.[20] Exteriors referred to the missions through construction materials—typically a roughcast cement stucco for the walls and barrel-shaped roof tiles—and such elements as scalloped gable parapets and dormers, colonnaded porches, and pergolas. The Mission (or Moorish, as it was then called) Revival style was initially used in hotels and railroad stations, such as the Hotel Ponce de León (now Flagler College) in Saint Augustine, Florida (1887), and Southern Pacific Station in Burlington, California (1894), but by the early 1900s was also used for houses. In rare cases, the overall form of the church was applied to residential design (fig. 5).

For the most part, however, the Mediterranean house in America through the 1920s sought not to replicate a particular precedent but to draw specific features from a variety of architectural models—Italian, Spanish, and Southwestern adobe being the most popular—and adapt them to American house types. Perhaps the earliest to integrate several Mediterranean sources was the James Waldron Gillespie house, built in Montecito, California, in 1902–6 (fig. 6). After seven months' travel

*Fig. 5* Charles Brigham. Burrage house, Redlands, California. 1901. Archives of the A. K. Smiley Public Library, Redlands

*Fig. 6* Bertram Grosvenor Goodhue. James Waldron Gillespie house, Montecito, California. 1902–6. Smithsonian Institution, Washington, D.C., Archives of American Gardens, Alfred Branum Collection. Property of Eleanor C. Weller

throughout Persia and Italy with architect Bertram Grosvenor Goodhue, Gillespie asked him to design a Roman pavilion set within gardens that referenced Persian and Italian landscape traditions.[21] Goodhue borrowed the Italian villa's courtyard plan and solid, minimally ornamented walls and the Persian garden's linear orientation; he also incorporated exotic interiors, such as a gold-leaf "Persian" room and a domed "Turkish" bathing room.

Charles Platt undertook a similar synthesis as he gravitated from landscape to architectural design, basing his early residential projects on an Americanized version of the Italian villa. He set the rustic villa's low-pitched hipped roof with exposed eaves on top of a form derived from the typical New England farmhouse: a simple rectangular box sheathed with rough-cut horizontal boarding or textured cement stucco. (The earliest example of this was Platt's own home in Cornish, New Hampshire, which he built in 1890.[22]) He usually placed a classical pergola at the entrance and the garden side of the house to connect the dwelling to the outdoors (see William H. Rand Jr. House).[23] In their plans, however, Platt's houses had no relationship to Italian precedent, as they lacked courtyards and other indoor/outdoor spaces. Essentially the same plan could have been used for an English Tudor or a Georgian Colonial house.

*Fig. 7*　J. Floyd Yewell. Drawing for "Mediterranean House."
*House & Garden*, July 1928

Like Platt, other architects began selecting from a broad menu of Mediterranean-inspired features. For example, the house designed by J. Floyd Yewell for *House & Garden* in 1928 has a simple rectangular form capped by a hipped roof, elements usually associated with Italian sources, but it also draws from Spanish and Southwestern adobe traditions (fig. 7). Its U-shaped plan wraps around a central court, which Yewell considered the house's focal point: "Of all the architectural features transported from Spain to our American semi-tropics, the patio is the most striking."[24] Spanish tile covers the roof and ornaments a courtyard wall fountain. Most of the house is contained in two stories, but the living room and adjacent bedroom are located within a simple, cubic one-story volume that references the Southwestern adobe; its roof, capped by a flat parapet, serves as a porch for a second-story bedroom.

The interiors were not illustrated, but the article discussed possible design treatments. The furniture should be of "Italian or Spanish origin or reproductions of the same." The lack of distinction between European antiques and American reproductions is consistent with the design intent of the Mediterranean house: to capture an essential character, not to convey architectural purity, adapting details to suit an American audience. That attitude was echoed in advertisements for furniture and decorative items published in shelter magazines of the 1920s (fig. 8).

The early twentieth-century Mediterranean house often reflected not only a mix of European precedents but other contemporary design movements as well. Many were devoid of surface ornament, suggesting the influence of the Arts and Crafts movement. And the central courtyard plan—especially when surrounded by consistently spaced columns—expressed a rational order that was associated with both Beaux Arts classicism and the Arts and Crafts movement. The geometries of the courtyard were sometimes used as the basis for the layout of the rest of the house, underscoring the plan's coherence. Such was the case at both the Santa Barbara estate Francis T. Underhill based on an eight-foot modular (see Solana) and the San Diego house Irving J. Gill designed for Henry and Edith Timken in 1911.[25] Gill surrounded a large central court with corridors or loggias, laying simple concrete columns roughly six feet on center on three sides (fig. 9). In a second court (created as an open-air schoolroom for the Timken children), engaged piers, approximately ten feet on center, defined two sides of the space and framed three sides of a walled garden.

*Fig. 8*　"Simonds Individualism in Good Furniture" advertisement.
*Arts and Decoration*, September 1926

*Fig. 9*    Irving J. Gill. Henry H. Timken house, San Diego. 1911. Irving J. Gill Collection, Architecture & Design Collection, University Art Museum, University of California Santa Barbara

Outdoor living spaces such as walled gardens and courtyards became the defining feature of the Mediterranean style in America. As architectural critic Eloise Roorbach noted, in the West

> the court is the center of the home life. It is usually considered the first essential of a home plan, and when people who live in California begin to put on paper their cherished dream of a home, nine times out of ten, they first draw a square, saying: "This is to be the court." Then around the square they add as many rooms as their fancy suggests or their purse permits.[26]

The courtyard plan was equally popular along the East Coast, in subtropical regions like Florida. An early example there was Vizcaya, the James Deering estate in Miami. Built in 1914–16, it helped establish the Mediterranean style in South Florida (fig. 10). Beautifully sited on Biscayne Bay, it was designed as an American-style *villa suburbana* by architect F. Burrall Hoffman Jr. and designer Paul Chalfin; the extensive Italian gardens were the creation of Diego Suarez. Waterfront locations, recalling the Roman tradition of the seaside villa, were seen at other early Mediterranean houses, especially in the East. Among them were Modern Venice, the Havemeyer residence in Islip,

Long Island (Grosvenor Atterbury, architect, 1897–98), and Eagle's Nest, the William K. Vanderbilt Jr. residence in Centerport, Long Island (Warren and Wetmore, architects, 1910–30).

## The Evolution of the Spanish Style

The typical Spanish-style house of the early 1920s was inspired by a romantic image of the Iberian castle. Externally this was conveyed by breaking the house into a series of "episodes" that might include a tower, an arcade, and a wall with decoratively ornamented windows. The castle theme continued inside with a sweeping staircase (if the house was more than one story tall), carved wooden and/or wrought-iron details, and Spanish-style furniture, either antiques or readily available American reproductions. These houses sometimes had an awkward quality, as if the designers were creating stage sets rather than a three-dimensional concept that unified all the parts.

By the mid-1920s the Andalusian farmhouse supplanted the castle as the preferred prototype for the Spanish house in America, offering a welcome simplicity and overall horizontality. The style enjoyed great popularity in Southern California and the Southwest, which, like Andalusia, have an arid climate. One of the most important innovators of the

*Fig. 10*    Burrall Hoffman Jr. and Paul Chalfin. Vizcaya, Miami. 1914–16

*Fig. 11*    George Washington Smith. Craig Heberton house, Montecito, California. 1916.
Courtesy of Patricia Gebhard

*Fig. 12*    Carlos Maruri and Paul Belau. Gallery of the Presidential Palace, Havana, Cuba. 1920. Tomás Estrada Palma Collection, Cuban Heritage Collection, University of Miami Libraries, Coral Gables, Florida

Andalusian farmhouse in the United States was Santa Barbara architect George Washington Smith. Like Charles Platt, Smith had trained as an artist and studied painting in Europe, where he became enamored with the purity of modernism's geometry, which he linked to the cubic volumes he saw in the simple farmhouse.[27] He explored that idea when he returned to California after World War I, designing an Andalusian-style house with white walls and tile roofs in Montecito (fig. 11).

In Florida, the Iberian influence on residential design came not directly from Spain but via its former colonies in the Caribbean, especially Cuba, with which it shares a hot, humid climate. Over the course of hundreds of years, Cuba's architects and designers had adapted the transplanted Spanish architecture to a tropical environment. Many of the features were consistent with those found in the Andalusian house, but the second story was generally treated differently: In the grand houses of Havana, the height of the upper floor was raised to allow for better air circulation (fig. 12).

Much of the wall space was devoted to large window openings (five to six feet wide by ten to fifteen feet tall), covered by wooden shutters to protect against the elements and control ventilation and light. While windows were not always so large in Florida as in Cuba, opening up much of the second story and using blinds to control air circulation are common features (see Tre Fontane and Rosalie and Richard Alter House). Cuba was also the source for tile used in many Florida houses of the 1920s. George E. Merrick, founder of Coral Gables, Florida, mandated that tile from old Cuban houses be used, to imbue the community with an immediate historical character.

## Mediterranean Style in Community Development

The popularity of the Mediterranean house coincided with a period of unrivaled suburban growth throughout the nation. New communities like Shaker Heights, Ohio, and new suburban tracts in established East Coast cities, such as Baltimore's Roland Park, demonstrated successful town-planning principles that guided each community's master plan, the design of streets, parks, and other communal spaces, and the review of new construction. Most commonly, suburban neighborhoods of the late nineteenth and early twentieth centuries contained diverse residential styles, with stucco Spanish and Italian houses alongside Anglo-Colonial and English Tudor types, but some established a cohesive visual identity, either by mandating consistent architectural imagery or implicitly achieving it through the review process. Of those that did—whether to revitalize an existing town or to design a new one—a limited number chose the Mediterranean style as the architectural theme.

Santa Barbara, California, is among the established cities that sought to create a new, unified image based on Mediterranean precedents. In the early twentieth century, city planner Charles Mulford Robinson recommended redesigning the city to emphasize its most attractive features,[28] notably its location (between the Santa Ynez Mountains and the Pacific Ocean) and cultural heritage, as seen in buildings dating to the Spanish and Mexican colonial eras. Over time, historic preservation became part of a larger urban design program that included controls over new architecture, landscaping, and street plans.[29]

A few private developments initially demonstrated Santa Barbara's aspirations to be a "new Spain," but the public commitment took hold only after an earthquake in June 1925.[30] Much of downtown was severely damaged, including a number of historic buildings, notably the Franciscan Mission Santa Barbara. Margaret Knight Andrews and other civic-minded local women raised money to repair the church and help the city acquire the open land adjacent to it,[31] which became Mission Historical Park. Individual property owners also began building houses that reflected the community-wide image. Andrews, for example, commissioned a group of Mediterranean Revival houses on Plaza Rubio, across the street from Mission Santa Barbara (see Plaza Rubio Houses).

Among the all-new Mediterranean-style communities was Coral Gables, Florida, one of the country's first planned cities (figs. 13, 14, 15). In 1921 developer George Merrick formed a committee of gifted designers and architects, led by the illustrator Denman Fink, that ultimately selected a Mediterranean design vocabulary for Coral Gables. As Merrick explained,

> The natural setting of Miami, swept by the breezes from the Gulf Stream, made the climate identical with that along the shores of the Mediterranean. And so we decided to adopt the Mediterranean type of architecture. Our designs have been popularly classified as Spanish, but this is not a correct description. We have buildings and residences of Italian, Venetian, North African, and Malayan as well as of Spanish design, and plan to add to these Japanese and Chinese as well as ancient Grecian models.[32]

The group traveled "to the old countries and to the South Sea Islands in search of genuine types of buildings."[33] Merrick then urged his architects "to emulate but not duplicate . . . castles in Spain," which he thought would most appeal to prospective residents. Phineas Paist, the supervising architect, established a board of architects that reviewed all plans to maintain a high standard of design; this board functions in the same capacity to this day. Despite almost a century's growth, Coral Gables, with a tree-lined commercial district and distinctive, upscale residences, retains a cohesive Mediterranean image.

## Regionalism

By the mid-1920s, a small number of architects in California and Texas began looking for alternatives to Spanish and Italian designs as precedent for new domestic work, believing the "romantically designed Mediterranean houses necessitated too great a break with the background and traditions familiar to most Americans."[34] Even in regions with a strong Spanish heritage, the style began to be viewed as an exotic import, and architects started turning toward local vernacular design and construction. As Houston architect John F. Staub put it,

> Is it not wiser for us to seek inspiration in the architecture developed in our own climate with materials at hand and adjust it to the tastes and requirements of our day, rather than to force the adaptation of types derived in foreign environments . . . ?[35]

Staub and others took to the roads, exploring local architectural forms: nineteenth-century limestone cottages in San Antonio, whitewashed stone houses with metal roofs in the Texas hill country towns of Castroville and Fredericksburg, and sandstone and adobe brick houses across the Mexican border.[36] The regionalist architecture that emerged in Texas often incorporated details from those models but, more important, echoed their simplicity of form and responsiveness to climate, seen in the use of porches and balconies.[37]

Traditional adobe construction also informed regionalist architecture in parts of California that had been settled by the Spanish or Mexicans, giving rise to two new types: the one-story California

*Figs. 13, 14, 15*   Above left and right: Leonard Schultze and S. Fullerton Weaver. Biltmore Hotel, Coral Gables, Florida. 1926. Below: Phineas E. Paist and Denman Fink. Venetian Pool, Coral Gables, Florida. 1924

ranch house and the two-story Monterey house,[38] which used different materials—generally stucco (sometimes combined with board and batten) or double-frame walls—to create the illusion of thick masonry walls. Borrowing from the adobe tradition, both typically featured outdoor access to the rooms; plans one-room deep and wrapped around a courtyard; and low-pitched roofs extending beyond the wall plane and supported by simple piers or columns. The Monterey style's characteristic cantilevered balcony was the principal access for the second-story rooms. Interest in regionalism intensified in the 1930s, coupled by a decisive shift toward simplicity that was triggered by both the slowly growing influence of modernism and the country's overall ascetic mood. In the wake of the economic crash, architectural fashion had moved away from the ostentation typified by the grand Mediterranean villas of Palm Beach, Florida, with their extravagantly colored and textured plasterwork. Unadorned vernacular features such as pitched roofs and whitewashed brick made a comeback; it was the heyday of the Colonial Revival, which exerted an Anglicizing influence on the Mediterranean style.

Historic preservation was both a source for and a product of regionalism. Local and federal initiatives to document historic buildings (and also to supply employment for out-of-work architects and draftsmen during the Great Depression) produced measured drawings and photographs; most influential were those by the Historic American Building Survey (HABS), published in *Architectural Forum* between 1934 and 1937. Such efforts as the restoration of Virginia's Colonial Williamsburg in the 1920s and 1930s and the contemporaneous reconstruction of San Antonio's so-called Spanish Governor's Palace (1749–60) also instilled communities' pride in local history (figs. 16, 17). For San Antonians, the Governor's Palace became a "monument to their city's glorious past. . . . It encouraged citizens to embrace the Hispanic heritage of the city, and make it part of their own identity."[39] The project galvanized other preservation efforts by the San Antonio Conservation Society and had a lasting influence on the city's architectural development: It provided source material as late as the 1960s, when architect Chris Carson measured one of the palace's fireplaces while designing a new residence (see Marshall and Patricia Steves House).

*Figs. 16, 17*  Spanish Governor's Palace, San Antonio, Texas. 1749–60

*Fig. 18*   John Gaw Meem. John and Faith Meem house, near Santa Fe, New Mexico. 1936. Photograph by Ernest Knee. Courtesy of Nancy Meem Wirth

Also in the 1930s, interest in the vernacular Mexican house began taking root in America's border states. Mexico had been a source for tile and wrought iron for many Mediterranean houses in the 1920s, but Americans at that time tended to turn to Europe, not Central America, for travel and inspiration; another reason Mexico's

domestic architecture may have been overlooked was that few texts on the subject were then available.[40] But awareness of Mexico's modest houses mounted after architects began documenting the adobes of the Southwest and West, which had been constructed while those regions were under Mexican control. Publications such as *Early Mexican Houses* (1930), with its photographs and measured drawings, became important resources.[41] Adobes both north and south of the border wrapped around patios or courtyards and expressed a handmade simplicity in the wall construction and materials, but the Mexican examples displayed a greater range of materials, color, and decorative detail. The growing appeal of architectural simplicity also accorded with the increasingly prominent modernist aesthetic, with its emphasis on eliminating excess ornament and function dictating form. But the modernists, who rejected the use of historically inspired styles, viewed even regionalist architecture as derivative and antiquarian. A charge of inauthenticity became part of the "modernist critique of traditionalism"[42] that ultimately propelled regionalism toward modernism in art and architecture.

*Fig. 19*   R. M. Schindler. R. M. Schindler house, West Hollywood, California. 1921–22

That evolution can be seen in the work of John Gaw Meem, who modified a Southwestern house type that the Anasazi, Hispanic, and Anglo cultures had developed over the course of a thousand years with subtle gestures toward modernism. For his own residence, built outside Santa Fe in 1936, Meem built the walls with age-old local materials—stones from a nearby arroyo set in lime mortar—whereas a few years earlier he might have constructed them of adobe-colored cement stucco over adobe or hollowed clay tile (fig. 18).[43] The interior incorporated modern ideas of an open, interpenetrating space and simplified surface pattern and color.

## The Modernist Impulse

Such developments in regionalist architecture were part of a broader blurring of differences between traditional and modern architecture as the two design camps pursued increasingly similar goals. As architects Paul Robinson Hunter and Walter Reichardt explained, "A growing appreciation of the importance of comfort and workability has been met by a more intensive use of space and a greater flexibility in planning, and has brought about a departure from the concept of 'pure' style and a release from the forms of traditional architecture."[44] Mediterranean style also converged with modernism in its emphasis on fluid movement between indoors and outdoors—which grew increasingly seamless—and was stimulated by modernism's embrace of contemporary materials and technology.

In turn, one of the earliest, most radical, and most influential modernist works was itself indebted to the Mediterranean style and the

*Fig. 20*    Carlos B. Schoeppl. Irving J. Reuter house, Miami Beach, Florida. 1931. Reproduced in Carlos B. Schoeppl and Arnold Southwell, *A Florida Brochure* (Miami Beach: c. 1932)

adobe house. Drawing upon those traditions, the house Viennese-born architect R. M. Schindler built in Los Angeles (now West Hollywood) in 1921–22 achieved an unprecedented integration of interior and exterior space, pioneering an essential aspect of modernism (fig. 19). Each of its three interlocking L-shaped units, laid out like a pinwheel, defines a courtyard. The house turns its back to the street with concrete walls, but wide sliding doors, screenlike walls, and clerestory windows unite the open-plan interiors with the gardens. By meshing his architectural geometries with the outdoors, Schindler expanded upon the work a decade earlier of Irving Gill and others who treated architecture and landscape as a whole. The house further references the adobes of the Southwest, where Schindler had spent time, in its flat roof, patio fireplaces, and exposed wooden structure. In such details, and by breaking through conventional barriers to the outdoors, Schindler linked traditional and modern design and set a lasting example for residential architecture, particularly in dry, mild climates like California's.

Modernism's impact on traditional design varied according to geography and by architect. In South Florida, where the streamlined Moderne style was widely embraced in the 1930s and 1940s, Mediterranean houses gradually absorbed some of its features: The modernist machine aesthetic made the edges of wall planes crisper, replacing the handmade look of previous generations of buildings, and curvaceous or streamlined aerodynamics crept into architectural details, such as the wrought-iron gate of Carlos B. Schoeppl's Irving J. Reuter house in Miami Beach (fig. 20).[45]

Beginning in the late 1950s and continuing through the 1960s, a movement known as the New Formalism synthesized modern materials and technology with elements of the classical tradition. Edward Durell Stone was one of the best-known architects associated with this movement. In 1956 he designed a house in Dallas (fig. 21) that he described as evoking a "sense of the classical Pompeiian house, enclosed by high walls, with all rooms opening to courtyards."[46] Here Stone referenced the atrium—an age-old device for bringing nature inside—with an indoor swimming pool and a dining room platform floating above a square moat of water. He provided easy access to the outdoors—valued by the ancients and moderns alike—with sliding glass doors leading to a pool and terraces shielded by his signature concrete-block screen walls. And he expressed a modernist impulse in

*Fig. 21*  Edward Durell Stone. Mr. and Mrs. Bruno Graf house, Dallas. 1956. Photograph by
Vincent G. Lisanti. Courtesy of National Foundation for Imaging Excellence, New York

the open floor plan—the first floor is essentially a single large space—
and ample use of glass, steel, and concrete.

By the late 1960s and early 1970s, the pendulum began to swing
away from modernism, particularly the International style of starkly
geometric forms, often of glass and steel. As criticism mounted that
modernism was sterile and insensitive to its residents' needs, the Mediterranean house gained a fresh appreciation among architects. Stone
and others had illustrated the Mediterranean house's responsiveness to
a modernist interest in free interaction between interior and exterior;
it was able to strike a balance between the rationality of the grid and
the sensuous appeal of access to nature, addressing the need for both
private living spaces and socially oriented, informal exteriors.[47]

The Mediterranean style had also proven that—rather than being
wed to antiquarian styles—it was almost infinitely adaptable to changing architectural fashions. It attracted new adherents in the 1970s with
the rise of postmodernism, which incorporated historical references
within the context of modern design, as seen in Charles W. Moore's
1972–74 residence for Lee Burns in Los Angeles (fig. 22). Moore
rebutted the modernist criticism that inspiration from past and foreign sources resulted in only artifice and pastiche, arguing that such
precedents could inform truly modern works of merit.

*I find recollections to be of very special interest these days since for
decades we have been told that it is wrong to suggest in the things
we do some preexisting things we like, since that isn't modern.
This has left the whole realm of making some connection with the
past . . . to the Walt Disneys of this world, who make some very
interesting things but robbed us of a freer and more real chance to
make those connections ourselves.[48]*

*Fig. 22*  Charles Moore with Richard Chylinski. Lee Burns house,
Los Angeles. 1972–74. Photograph by John Nikolais. c. 1980.
Courtesy of Moore Ruble Yudell, Santa Monica, California

Fig. 23　Ralph Rapson. Greenbelt House design. Case Study House Program. 1945.
Courtesy of Ralph Rapson & Associates Inc., Minneapolis

For the Burns project, Moore borrowed elements of the Mediterranean house—including its stucco wall planes, multiple shed roofs, and courtyards—but recomposed them like a collage. Moore tended to organize his spaces vertically, and here he used a winding stair as a "device for overlapped and sensed space; an implication of flow rather than a simple notion of circulation."[49] The exterior is painted in warm tones, selected by designer Tina Beebe, that convey the character of a faded villa.

Barton Myers, who opened a Los Angeles office in 1984, even more fully infused the Mediterranean style with a modernist sensibility, addressing it with new materials and technology. Inspired by the Maison de Verre, built in Paris by Pierre Chareau and architect Bernard Bijvoet in 1928–31, and by later examples, Myers applied the creative potential of steel to residential work. As seen in earlier industrial and commercial buildings, steel's strength allows for a minimal structural skeleton, providing the transparency of floor-to-ceiling windows and broad column spans.[50] Myers explored its use in a house he built in Los Angeles in 2006, which consists of three pavilions of structural steel, glass, and aluminum almost completely open to a central courtyard (see Rick and Carmen Rogers House). In examining ways to open walls to the outdoors, it directly descends from R. M. Schindler's house and Ralph Rapson's Greenbelt House, an unbuilt 1945 design

for two steel or wood structures framing a roofed courtyard garden (fig. 23). While Schindler's essentially solid house with abundant glass and sliding doors was a pivotal work, Rapson's design for a light, open structure is the immediate antecedent to Myers's project.

Modern interpretations of the courtyard plan such as Myers's represent just one of the contemporary approaches to the Mediterranean house; other architects are exploring it in a more traditional vein. Jorge Hernandez of Coral Gables (fig. 24; see Rosalie and Richard Alter House) and Michael Imber of San Antonio are two gifted practitioners of traditional design. Imber's residential projects evoke local precedents of the 1920s, including the houses by Atlee and Rob-

Fig. 24　Jorge Hernandez. Drawing of "Tres Villas," Coral Gables, Florida.
1991. Courtesy of Jorge Hernandez, Coral Gables

*Fig. 25*    Michael Imber. Drawing of Daniell house, San Antonio, Texas. 2000. Courtesy of Michael G. Imber Architects, San Antonio

ert Ayres (see Percy L. Mannen House). The Daniell house, built in San Antonio in 2000 (fig. 25), recalls its predecessors in its restrained ornamentation and the devices used to break up the house's mass: the asymmetrical composition, the contrasts of solid and almost entirely open walls with arched French doors, and the distinction of various sections by different roof treatments (hipped, low-pitch gable, and almost flat). Like a number of the Ayreses' works, the Daniell house

pivots around a central element—a tower—not only to fragment the structure but to take advantage of air currents. It is indisputably a new construction, but one imbued with the lessons of architectural history.

The Mediterranean house has proven remarkably resilient, adapting to changes in architectural fashion throughout the twentieth century and into the twenty-first. While the earliest interpretations of the house and its lush landscape captured an idyllic view of the Old World, the style's longevity stems from characteristics sympathetic to the tenets of modern design: an overall simplicity of form and the seamless integration of indoor and outdoor living spaces. Those same qualities lend Mediterranean houses an ease and a gracious informality—what one historian called "a family atmosphere composed of solid, familiar things"[51]—that continue to be attractive to homeowners and relevant to contemporary architecture.

The following pages examine the style's evolution through twenty-five of the finest Mediterranean Revival houses built across the United States over the past hundred years. Collectively they illustrate why, through decades of change and dramatically different variations, the appeal of the Mediterranean endures.

1. Michael McDonough, "Selling Sarasota: Architecture and Propaganda in a 1920s Boom Town," *Journal of Decorative and Propaganda Arts* 23 (1998), Florida theme issue, 11–31.

2. Helen I. Kohen, "Perfume, Postcards, and Promises: The Orange in Art and Industry," *Journal of Decorative and Propaganda Arts* 23 (1998), Florida theme issue, 33–47.

3. Fox, *Spanish-Mediterranean Houses of Houston*, 9–10.

4. On the Mission Revival, Karen J. Weitze, *California's Mission Revival* (Los Angeles: Hennessey & Ingalls, 1984); Thomas Graham, "Henry M. Flagler's Hotel Ponce de Leon," *Journal of Decorative and Propaganda Arts* 23 (1998), Florida theme issue, 96–111.

5. Rexford Newcomb, *Mediterranean Domestic Architecture in the United States* (New York: Acanthus Press, reprint 1999), n. p. Architectural critic Henry Saylor added the country house of southern France to the mixture. Henry H. Saylor, "The Mediterranean Influence," *Garden and Home Builder* 44:3 (November 1926), 207; and Henry H. Saylor, "The Mediterranean Influence," in Lucy Embury Hubbell, *The Book of Little Houses* (Garden City, N.Y.: Doubleday, Page & Co., 1927), 15.

6. See Mark Alan Hewitt, "Rich Men and Their Houses," in *The Architect and the Country House, 1890–1940* (New Haven and London: Yale University Press, 1990), 1–23. Karl Baedeker's numerous guidebooks to European countries included references to the great houses that were open to the American public, e.g., *Italy from the Alps to Naples* (Leipzig: Karl Baedeker Publisher, 1928). Robert Nathan Cram, "The Important Italian Villas: A Brief Guide," *House Beautiful*, June 1926, 814.

7. David Gebhard, "The Myth and the Power of Place: Hispanic Revivalism in the American Southwest," in Nicholas C. Markovich and Wolfgang F. E. Preiser, eds., *Pueblo Style and Regional Architecture* (New York: Van Nostrand Reinhold, 1992), 143–47.

8. Wharton, 41.

9. Ibid., 46.

10. Morgan, 35.

11. An early example of this generation of American architects' interest in Italian precedent is McKim, Mead & White's Villard Houses (New York, 1882–85).

12. Matthew Digby Wyatt, *An Architect's Notebook in Spain* (London: Autotype Fine Art Company, 1872); A. C. Michael, *An Artist in Spain* (London and New York: Hodder and Stoughton, 1914).

13. In 1933 J. Paul Getty purchased Joaquín Sorolla y Bastida's 1910 painting *Corner of the Garden, Alcazar, Sevilla* (fig. 3). He later wrote: "I was struck by the remarkable quality of Sorolla's paintings, being especially fascinated by his unique treatment of sunlight." (www.getty.edu/art/gettyguide/artObjectDetails?artobj=811, September 16, 2007). Sorolla's work was the subject of the inaugural exhibition of the Hispanic Society of America in New York, a museum and library founded in 1909 by Archer Milton Huntington and today an important repository of Spanish art, artifacts, and manuscripts.

14. Nineteenth-century literary accounts of interest in this region and its Moorish history include Washington Irving's *Alhambra* (Philadelphia: Carey & Lea, 1832).

15. Elizabeth Leonard Strang, "The Making of a Spanish-American Garden," *House Beautiful* XLIV:2 (July 1918), 94–95, 103; Helen Morganthau Fox, "Spanish Ideas for American Gardens," *Ladies Home Journal* XLVII:3 (March 1930), 157, 160; Mildred Stapley Byne, *Spanish Gardens and Patios* (Philadelphia & London: J. B. Lippincott Company; New York: The Architectural Record, 1924).

16. A. T. Grove and Oliver Rackham, "Cultivation Terraces," in *The Nature of Mediterranean Europe, an Ecological History* (New Haven and London: Yale University Press, 2001), 107–17.

17. James S. Ackerman, *The Villa: Form and Ideology of Country Houses* (Princeton, N.J.: Princeton University Press, 1990), 42–43.

18. See Ernesto De Carolis, "A City and Its Rediscovery," in Annamaria Ciarallo and Ernesto De Carolis, *Pompeii: Life in a Roman Town* (Milan: Electa, 1999), 23–30.

19. As a young man Goodhue traveled to Mexico and wrote about his experiences in *Mexican Memories* (1892). He also provided the floor plans accompanying Sylvester Baxter's twelve-volume study, *Spanish-Colonial Architecture in Mexico* (Boston: J. B. Millet, 1901). He argued that this background made him the best-qualified architect to design the buildings for the Panama-California Exposition in San Diego (1911–15).

20. David Gebhard, "The Spanish Colonial Revival in Southern California (1895–1930)," *Journal of the Society of Architectural Historians* 26:2 (May 1967), 131–47.

21. Romy Wyllie, *Bertram Goodhue, His Life and Residential Architecture* (New York: W. W. Norton & Co., 2007), 42–51; David Gebhard, "The Mediterranean Villa in America: Three Episodes," 43–45.

22. Morgan, 26–27.

23. Ibid., 48.

24. "From the Mediterranean to America," *House & Garden* 54:1 (July 1928), 56.

25. Thomas S. Hines, *Irving Gill and the Architecture of Reform* (New York: The Monacelli Press, 2000), 112–14; Bruce Kamerling, *Irving J. Gill, Architect* (San Diego: San Diego Historical Society, 1993), 78–79.

26. Eloise Roorbach, "Outdoor Life in California Houses, as Expressed in the New Architecture of Irving J. Gill," *The Craftsman*, July 1913 (www.irvinggill.com/roorbach-gill.html#anchorcraftsman1913).

27. John Taylor Boyd, "Houses Showing a Distinguished Simplicity," *Arts & Decoration* 33 (October 1930), 57.

28. Charles Mulford Robinson, *The Report of Charles Mulford Robinson Regarding the Civic Affairs of Santa Barbara, California* (printed for the Civic League by the *Independent*, 1909).

29. For the history of design review in Santa Barbara, see David Gebhard, "Introduction," in Conard and Nelson, 9–23.

30. David Gebhard, *Santa Barbara: The Creation of a New Spain in America*, 23.

31. Mary Louise Days, "Margaret Knight Forsyth Andrews," unpublished ms., collection of author, June 11, 1987, 7. This is the most thorough source on the history of Mrs. Andrews's contribution to Santa Barbara.

32. Chambers, 20.

33. Ibid.

34. Paul Robinson Hunter and Walter Reichardt, *Residential Architecture in Southern California: Mediterranean to Modern 1939* (Los Angeles: Hennessey & Ingalls, 1998 reprint of 1939 edition), 27.

35. John F. Staub, "Latin Colonial Architecture in the Southwest," *Civics for Houston* 1 (February 1928), 6.

36. Architect Roland E. Coate wrote of pulling off the road to visit an "old adobe" north of San Diego in "Capturing Some of California's Romance," *California Southland* 7 (May 1925), 24.

37. David R. Williams, "An Indigenous Architecture: Some Texas Colonial Houses," *Southwest Review* 14 (October 1928), 60–74. See Papademetriou, 36–41; Donald R. Hannaford and Revel Edwards, *Spanish Colonial or Adobe Architecture of California, 1800–1859* (New York: Architectural Book Publishing Company, Inc., 1931); Fox, *The Country Houses of John F. Staub*.

38. For a discussion of the California ranch house see David Bricker, "Ranch Houses Are Not All Alike," www.nps.gov/history/NR/publications/bulletins/suburbs/Bricker.pdf. On the Monterey house see David Gephard, "The Monterey Tradition History Reordered," *New Mexico Studies in the Fine Arts* 7 (1982), 14–19, and "Some Additional Observations on California's Monterey Tradition," *Journal of the Society of Architectural Historians* 46 (June 1987), 157–70.

39. Kenneth Hafertepe, "The Romantic Rhetoric of the Spanish Governor's Palace, San Antonio, Texas," *Southwestern Historical Quarterly* 17:2 (October 2003), 275. Harvey P. Smith was the restoration architect. Much of his work was based on material evidence, but other spaces were built on conjecture. Additionally, it is more likely that this was the residence of the presidio commander rather than the governor.

40. David Gebhard, "Introduction," in Richard Garrison and George W. Rustay's *Early Mexican Houses* (New York: Architectural Book Publishing Company, Inc., 1990 reprint of 1930 edition), xii.

41. Richard Garrison and George W. Rustay, *Early Mexican Houses* (New York: Architectural Book Publishing Company, Inc., 1990 reprint of 1930 edition).

42. Stephen Fox, "Dallas Modern: A Perspective on the Modern Movement in Dallas," *Architecturally Significant Homes* (www.dougnewby.com/architecture/styles/stephen_fox.asp, June 20, 2007).

43. Chris Wilson, *Facing Southwest: The Life and Houses of John Gaw Meem* (New York: W. W. Norton & Company, 2001), 164.

44. Hunter and Reichardt, 69.

45. Carlos B. Schoeppl and Arnold Southwell, *A Florida Brochure* (Miami Beach, Fla.: self published, c. 1932).

46. Edward Durell Stone, *Evolution of an Architect* (New York: Horizon Press, 1962), 141

47. Katherine Liapi and Charles W. Moore, "Courtyard Living," *Ah Mediterranean! Twentieth Century Classicism in America, Center* 2 (1986), 78–89.

48. Charles Moore, "Architecture and Fairy Tales," in James Steele, ed., *Moore Ruble Yudell* (London: Academy Editions, 1993), 16.

49. Paul Heyer, *American Architecture: Ideas and Ideologies in the Late Twentieth Century* (New York: Van Nostrand Reinhold, 1993), 37.

50. Esther McCoy, *Case Study Houses, 1945–1962*, 2nd ed. (Los Angeles: Hennessey & Ingalls, 1977); Elizabeth A. T. Smith, ed., *Blueprints for Modern Living: History and Legacy of the Case Study House* (Los Angeles: Museum of Contemporary Art; Cambridge, Mass.: MIT Press, 1998); Elizabeth A. T. Smith, *Case Study Houses* (Köln and New York: Taschen, c. 2002).

51. Eglo Benincasa, "Houses in the Sun: The Mediterranean Tradition," *Landscape* 6:1 (Autumn 1956), 18.

# William H. Rand Jr. House

✤

Above: East porch. Opposite: Entrance

**A KEY FIGURE IN THE EVOLUTION OF THE MEDITERRANEAN REVIVAL HOUSE**
was artist-turned-architect Charles Platt, who pioneered the physical and visual integration of the dwelling and garden that is
its defining characteristic.

Following the 1894 publication of his *Italian Gardens*, the first American book on the subject,[1] Platt received several commissions to install Italian gardens at existing houses in New England (see fig. 2 in Introduction), as well as projects to design
new houses where he could explore his concept of the American villa. He integrated the simplicity of the wood-frame and
wood-sheathed New England farmhouse with features associated with the analogous building type in Italy: hipped roofs, overhanging eaves, and loggias supported by columns.[2] In his view, America was ready for country houses modeled on the Italian
villa and its classical landscape.

> *The habit of life of the people in the United States is distinctly congenial to the villa idea. The winters are spent in the city and the*
> *summers in the country. Men go to the country for recreation, health, and pleasure, while in the city they leave their real interests,*
> *business, etc. Climate leads them to be as much as possible out of doors in the summer. The country houses should be extended*
> *and the scheme of gardens, terraces, etc., which does this in the Italian villas can be applied here. It seems not improbable that*
> *within the next generation or so this country may be the centre of development in villa design.[3]*

Platt's comments proved prescient. The early decades of the twentieth century saw unprecedented construction of country houses, because of both growing affluence and modern transportation systems that were making suburban locations ever more accessible. About twenty miles north of New York City, the village of Rye was undergoing a construction boom that followed the completion in 1904 of a trolley line connecting it to the city.

Platt's house for William H. Rand Jr. (1903–4) was among the new buildings in Rye at that time. He may have designed it as a summer house for city dwellers,[4] as it was relatively modest in size compared with nearby estates.[5] It beautifully demonstrates how Platt subtly adapted the principles of the Italian villa and its garden into American country house design. The two-story brick house lacks the central courtyard typical of true Mediterranean houses, but its overall imagery is Mediterranean, including the lightly troweled cement stucco sheathing, hipped roof with exposed rafters, and simple wooden columns supporting the entrance and garden porches.

Platt believed "symmetry or its effect was essential to a beautiful building,"[6] and he applied this dictate to the Rand house as well. The central sections of the principal facades are symmetrical, and the lateral wings are balanced, though not identical. Though symmetry often begets formality, the house has a relaxed feel, partly because Platt let nature prevail. Views of the garden are pervasive within the house. From the entry, it can be glimpsed through a pair of glazed

Opposite: Entry hall. Above: Garden view

French doors at the end of the hall, and the principal rooms—the parlor (living room) and study to the right of the hall and the dining room to the left—all have windows facing the garden.

Graciously proportioned, well lit, and comfortable, the principal rooms are paneled with wood—another Platt signature, although fluted piers and pilasters, moldings, and mantels generally reference an Anglo-Colonial classicism rather than anything remotely Italian. Altogether, the interior design suggests that of a traditional Colonial.

The key components of the site plan are the house, the formal garden immediately east of the house, the view from the garden, and the service areas. Platt drew a clear west-east axis from the entrance porch,

through the hallway, the larger eastern porch, and the garden to a vista with a large meadow beyond. That orientation capitalizes on the site's natural characteristics, including native trees (cedar, wild cherry, hickory, apple, elm, and several varieties of oaks) along the southern and eastern sides and a concealed ledge east of the garden, beyond which the property drops precipitously. The land also drops more gradually to the northeast, enabling Platt to slightly obscure the view of the service building—a wooden stable (now a garage).

The original plan for the garden consisted of a central lawn with a large semicircular terminus at its eastern side and flower beds to the north and south; today a pool replaces the central lawn. The principal

Above: Parlor. Below: Dining room

access to the garden remains the large eastern porch, which functions as an outdoor room. Low walls lightly enclose the garden along its northern and southern edges, and the eastern edge is enclosed by a pergola that echoes the details of the porch. Characteristic of Platt, the garden includes Italian sculptural elements, including a birdbath and large planters of topiary.

The house's integration with the landscape reflects Platt's commitment to the villa tradition, but the overall design suggests a synthesis of vernacular traditions and Platt's own design principles, lightly "dusted" by Latinized references. By introducing Mediterranean elements in this way, Platt played a pivotal role in making the style accessible to Americans, rendering it familiar rather than exotic.

1. See Morgan, 24–62.

2. Ibid., 47.

3. Russell Sturgis, *A Dictionary of Architecture and Building*, vol. 3 (Detroit: Gale Research Co., 1966 reprint of 1902 edition), 1,904.

4. At this writing, biographical information about Rand is inconclusive.

5. *Atlas of Westchester County, N.Y. Pocket, Desk and Automobile Edition*, vol. 1 (New York: G. W. Bromley & Co., 1914), 246.

6. Morgan, 80.

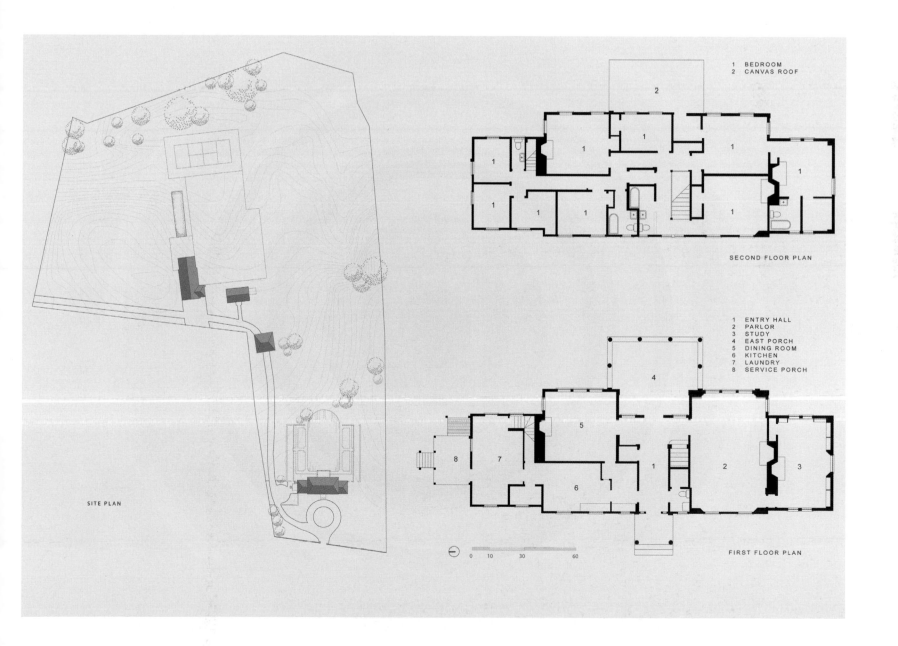

SITE PLAN

1 BEDROOM
2 CANVAS ROOF

SECOND FLOOR PLAN

1 ENTRY HALL
2 PARLOR
3 STUDY
4 EAST PORCH
5 DINING ROOM
6 KITCHEN
7 LAUNDRY
8 SERVICE PORCH

0    10        30              60

FIRST FLOOR PLAN

# ANDREW
# LAWSON
# HOUSE

Above: Dining room. Opposite: Staircase. Overleaf: Living room

IN THE EARLY TWENTIETH CENTURY, AMERICAN RESIDENTIAL DESIGN
responded to the Mediterranean tradition in two distinct ways: through adaptation of Italian gardens (but not yet Italian
houses), guided by the writings and practices of Charles Platt, Guy Lowell, Edith Wharton, and others; and by embracing the
Mission Revival, which emerged most strongly in California and Florida. The two rarely came together into a unified scheme;
the gardens drew upon a sophisticated European model, while the architecture was based on a more rustic colonial variant.
Among the alternatives found by designers seeking a cohesive approach to the house and its garden was the Pompeiian house,
which could be adapted to a waterfront or a garden setting.

The Pompeiian house type was one of the earliest in Western architecture to incorporate landscape within and adjacent to
a dwelling's perimeter walls. Archaeological excavations of Pompeii had unearthed houses both in town and in nearby suburbs.
The urban houses typically had blank side walls and a spatial orientation flowing toward the rear. Suburban houses, such as the
Villa of the Mysteries, though on larger sites, did not sprawl across the landscape. Like the urban houses, the suburban ones
had solid walls and both visual and physical links to the outdoors.

The Andrew Lawson house, completed in Berkeley, California, in 1908, was architect Bernard Maybeck's great inter-
pretation of the Pompeiian house. Maybeck's innovations sprang from his knowledge of the past. He had attended the
École des Beaux-Arts, where studies of Pompeiian houses were an established exercise, and he was fascinated by ruins.
Landscape architecture historian Dianne Harris has written about Maybeck's interest in Piranesi's eighteenth-century

engravings of Roman ruins, which may have included his series the Antiquités de Pompeïa (1804–7).[1]

The choice of a Pompeiian precedent may have been Maybeck's response to the allure the Mediterranean character of California's landscape held for him: In his drawings, he unified architecture and landscape through filtered golden light that evokes an Arcadian dream. Maybeck likewise warmed up the Lawson house walls with soft colors: The upper portions are painted buff, and the lower portions are pink (one of Maybeck's favorite wall colors). He introduced a sgraffito panel on the east facade of the second floor, surrounding the arches of a sleeping porch. Coupled with the tinted walls, it enlivens and ages the building. Trellises resting on engaged piers, window boxes, and a pergola are additional devices Maybeck used to link the house with its landscaped setting and to fragment its appearance to convey a sense of age.

The house is sited near the northern property line, allowing space for an extensive terraced landscape that follows the southern and eastern slopes of the land. Interior circulation on the first floor progresses from a modest entrance (on the north facade) through a richly ornamented stair hall. The hall provides access to the womblike billiards room and kitchen on either side; south of the kitchen it dramatically opens to merge with the dining room, which opens to the garden terrace, and a more enclosed living room. The latter is divided into a reading area and an alcove framed by a low arch, which provides intimate seating adjacent to an overscale fireplace. The interiors take full advantage of the magnificent views of Berkeley and the San Francisco Bay beyond. Currently the walls are painted in warm earth tones, and many are adorned by art created by owner Nancy Genn. On the second floor, five bedrooms access three sleeping porches, facilitating contact with the outdoors. Arched openings frame the porches on the east and west facades, while the southern porch has a more formal presence, with engaged piers capped by trellises.

The house is constructed of poured-in-place reinforced concrete, rarely used for single-family houses at the time (in fact, such use remains atypical). It is likely that Andrew Lawson—a world-famous geologist—was responsible for its selection. Soon after his arrival in California, Lawson identified the San Andreas Fault. While he saw no immediate danger, it was along this fault line that a devastating earthquake struck in 1906. In the quake's aftermath, Lawson authored a major study that included recommendations about rebuilding in seismic zones.[2] At about

Above: Bedroom with sleeping porch. Below: Bedroom with sleeping porch, bathroom

the same time he purchased land to build a house in Berkeley, but soon thereafter learned that the main trace of another fault ran through it. To forestall the destruction he'd witnessed after the San Andreas earthquake, he chose to use reinforced concrete for both its relative ability to withstand seismic activity and its fire resistance.

Maybeck may have been equally enthusiastic about the material.[3] His work expressively uses concrete, most notably in Berkeley's First Church of Christ Scientist (1910), and in the Lawson house it represents pure form. Frank Lloyd Wright's Unity Temple in Oak Park, Illinois (1908), and his fireproof house for the *Ladies Home Journal* in 1907 likewise demonstrate concrete construction's ability to convey geometric purity. To articulate and ornament his monolithic design for Lawson, Maybeck embedded small tiles in the concrete and incised its upper-floor surfaces with a diamond-shaped diaper pattern. Score lines surround the door and window openings, emphasizing their geometry.

Because of the expense of concrete construction ($17,533, equivalent to more than $365,000 in 2008), the architect eliminated some of the more elaborate materials he originally planned to use. For example, he replaced the Caen stone imported from France he'd intended for the stairway with integrally colored black concrete with gilt glass tesserae.[4] He used a scrolled motif for his cast plaster stair railings. Displaying such inventiveness throughout the house and in his use of concrete, "Maybeck transformed ordinary materials into art."[5]

---

1. Harris, 100.

2. John Dvorak, "Andrew Lawson: Discoverer of the San Andreas Fault," *The World & I Online Magazine*, www.worldandi.com, January 14, 2008.

3. Maybeck used two grades of concrete: a "rich mixture" made of one part cement, two parts sand, and four parts rock, and a "poorer mixture" with one part cement, three parts sand, and six parts rock. The rich mixture was used for floors, roofs, stairs, beams, and girders; the poorer mixture for walls and partitions. "Specifications for the Reinforced Concrete Work for the Residence of Professor A. C. Lawson," November 6, 1907. Maybeck Collection, Environmental Design Archives, University of California, Berkeley.

4. Woodbridge, 122.

5. Ibid.

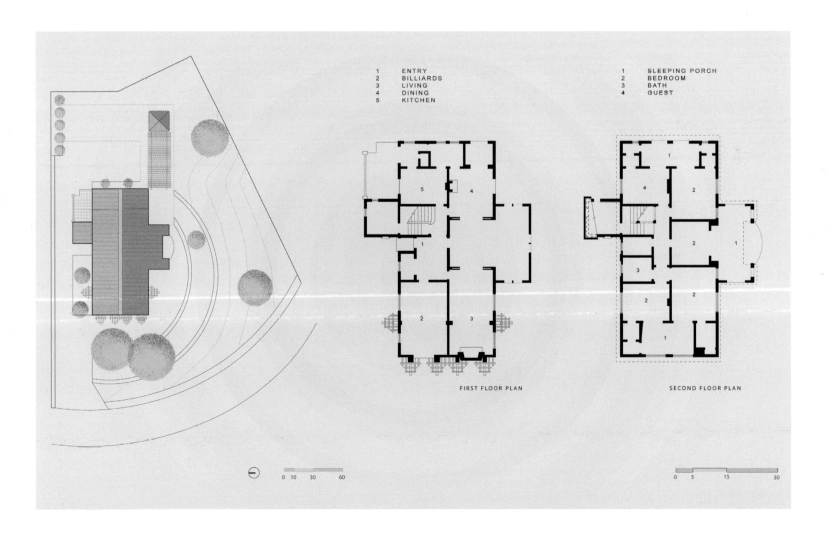

| 1 | ENTRY |
| 2 | BILLIARDS |
| 3 | LIVING |
| 4 | DINING |
| 5 | KITCHEN |

| 1 | SLEEPING PORCH |
| 2 | BEDROOM |
| 3 | BATH |
| 4 | GUEST |

FIRST FLOOR PLAN    SECOND FLOOR PLAN

0  10   30      60

0   5    15    30

# Solana

*Frederick Forest and*

*Sarah Griffith Peabody House*

Above: Lily pond. Opposite: View from courtyard to entry hall

# THE FIRST VIEW OF SOLANA ("SUNNY PLACE")—WITH ITS DRAMATIC

juxtaposition of ornamental entry and severely simple walls—reveals the masterful hand of its designer, Francis T. Underhill. He was not a trained architect but apparently developed his ability through extensive travel and keen observation; his minimalist treatment of this 1915 Santa Barbara (originally Montecito) estate reveals his awareness of contemporary innovations in American and European architecture. He was ahead of his time too in conceiving Solana's architecture and landscape as a fully unified composition, using the lush and varied landscape as a foil for the architecture's simplicity and to belie the rational order of its gridlike plan.

Because he worked largely in the Santa Barbara area, Underhill has not received the wide recognition his talent deserves. He moved to California from the East in the 1880s and began designing projects for his family and friends. By 1910 he had an architecture office in Montecito.[1]

The owners of Solana, Frederick Forest and Sarah Griffith Peabody, likewise were transplanted Easterners.[2] A self-made man, Frederick Peabody transformed a Troy, New York, manufacturer of shirts, collars, and cuffs into the extraordinarily successful firm of Cluett, Peabody & Co., owners of Arrow shirts. Beginning in 1906, on his second visit to the area, he began acquiring land in Montecito, eventually purchasing a total of seventy-nine acres.[3]

Peabody hired Charles F. Eaton, a gifted landscape architect and a central figure of the local Arts and Crafts scene, to develop the grounds. Another landscape architect, Peter Riedel, was subsequently engaged to landscape the property.

Above: Archival view of north loggia. c. 1915. Santa Barbara (Calif.) Historical Museum. Right: North loggia today

Peabody and Riedel added many trees to the existing oaks: seven thousand eucalyptus trees, begun as seedlings, mature orange trees, a palm weighing twelve tons, and a giant, twenty-ton rubber tree.[4] In June 1911 the local newspaper reported that Underhill was making drawings for Peabody's residence. It was described as mission style, with a plastered exterior, a concrete foundation, concrete porches with concrete columns, and a tile roof. The cost was estimated at five thousand dollars.[5] When the building permit was issued in 1913, the house was valued at fifty thousand dollars and the garage another three thousand dollars[6]—a price driven high by the cost of concrete.

Underhill located the house at the highest point of the property, with a long drive leading to it from the road. In front of the house is a large, rectangular entrance court that affords panoramic views from the Pacific Ocean to the Santa Ynez Mountains. The house stands at the east end of the court; its severe entrance facade is magnificently balanced by the lush nature before it. Two wings project from what appears to be a one-story house. (In fact, a partial lower floor is nestled against the hillside that drops to the south.) A string course reiterates the horizontality of the facade, which is broken only by a large, glazed terra-cotta door surround. Several varieties of palm trees and Italian cypress frame the facade and the marble steps leading to the front door.

Underhill's decision to treat the facade as a solid, protective wall reflects the Spanish urban design tradition, with a defensive exterior allowing for the interior to flow safely and easily to the outdoors. The principal floor is organized around a central courtyard, which in turn surrounds a large oak; today palms and other semitropical plants make

it an inviting outdoor room. The courtyard's eastern wall is solid; a shell-shaped niche holds a sculpture of a woman. The loggias running around the three other sides originally were open, linking the house to its outdoor sanctuary, but were subsequently enclosed with arched glass doors, creating gallery space for the owners' art collection. Massive Tuscan columns run along two sides of the courtyard, echoed by a pair of columns in the reception hall that visually connects the entry with it. Sited eight foot on center, the columns articulate the consistent grid that governs the entire house's floor plan.

Architectural historian David Gebhard observed that regardless of the style or size of Underhill's projects, they "convey an Arts and Crafts atmosphere in their simple, rational, and direct plans and through their unadorned interior and exterior surfaces."[7] Gebhard suggested that Underhill's use of "Cubistic plaster volumes," evident at Solana, brought his houses "close to the simplicity that we associate with the concurrent work of Irving J. Gill"—for example, the 1911 Henry H. Timken house in San Diego (see fig. 9 in Introduction). By eliminating surface ornament and other arguably extraneous features (such as tile-covered roof overhangs), Gill and Underhill developed a pared-down aesthetic that paralleled the contemporary work of the Vienna Secession movement.[8]

The principal rooms are at the house's eastern end, where a spacious living room is flanked by the dining room and library. A bowed wall of

Living room

French doors leads from the living room to a large terrace, whose shape repeats the curve of the living room wall. The dining room windows face the ocean and the garden, while the library is much darker and more intimate, with a view of an ancient oak and the mountains.

A number of changes were made to other rooms about 2005 in response to previous insensitive alterations and a fire in the northern half of the house.[9] Architect Don Nulty echoed Underhill's understated forms and sensitivity to the site while responding to the current owners' need to accommodate numerous guests. The northern portion now includes a reception room; the oak paneling there came from a seventeenth-century French château and was purchased from the William Randolph Hearst Collection. Beyond this are guest bedrooms and baths, and a terrace offering views of the mountains. Nulty also designed a guesthouse at the west end of the entrance court.

On the house's south side, where the master bedroom suite, kitchen, pantry, and dining room are, Nulty greatly improved access to the outdoors. A pergola-covered terrace runs the full length and includes intimate eating areas at each end; the one to the west connects by steps to the main, grandly scaled rear terrace, which offers sweeping views. The rear facade synthesizes the house's primary design elements, reiterating the Tuscan columns and the curve of the wall.

Bedroom

Above: Terrace overlooking Pacific Ocean. Below: Courtyard

In the extensive gardens Underhill designed an arch-shaped pool (now used as a lily pond) that repeats the curve of the house and rear terrace. It was fitted with a hydraulically operated platform designed to support an orchestra. A rose garden has been established where the Peabodys had seating for an amphitheater.

Solana is a complex and pioneering interpretation of the Mediterranean house. It was radical for its simplicity of form, its clear and consistent plan, and its early integration of architecture and landscape. It's a work of immense importance to the history of the Mediterranean house and, more broadly, American country house design.

1. David Gebhard, "Francis T. Underhill," 105.

2. The Peabodys, who had five children, divorced in 1918. In 1920 Frederick Peabody married Katherine Burke, who had been a Red Cross volunteer during World War I. "Santa Barbara's Most Decorated Woman," "Solana" file, Montecito History Room, Montecito (Calif.) Branch Library. Upon her death in 1959, sixteen acres of Solana's grounds were donated to the city of Santa Barbara for a public park, which was named in her honor.

3. Once Peabody established residency in Montecito, he was an active participant and philanthropist in many city institutions, including public schools, Cottage Hospital, Lobero Theater, and Ocean Front City Park. "Stroke Proves Fatal to Mr. Peabody and Death Takes Civic Benefactor," *Santa Barbara Daily News*, Feb. 24, 1927, Section 2, 9–10.

4. "F. F. Peabody" File, Gledhill Library, Santa Barbara Historical Society.

5. "Off Beat" clippings, "Solana" file, Montecito History Room, Montecito (Calif.) Branch Library.

6. Myrick, 335.

7. David Gebhard, "Francis T. Underhill," 106.

8. See David Gebhard, "The Spanish Colonial Revival in Southern California (1895–1930)," *Journal of the Society of Architectural Historians* 26:2 (May 1967), 140, 142.

9. From 1959 to 1979 Solana was owned by the Center for the Study of Democratic Institutions, which was created in response to the abuse of American civil liberties in the McCarthy era. The organization held conferences and published studies on such topics as integration, academic freedom, and national security. Among the luminaries invited were John F. Kennedy, Martin Luther King Jr., William O. Douglas, and Henry Kissinger. "Guide to the Center for the Study of Democratic Institutions Collection, 1950–1991," MS 18, Special Collections, Davidson Library, University of California Santa Barbara; Michael Redmon, "What is the History of the Center for the Study of Democratic Institutions," *The Independent*, June 5, 2002.

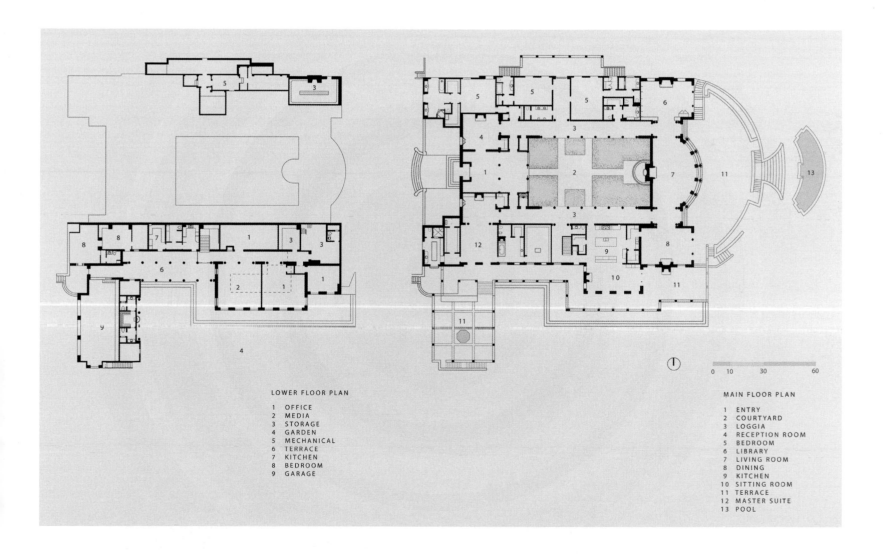

LOWER FLOOR PLAN

1 OFFICE
2 MEDIA
3 STORAGE
4 GARDEN
5 MECHANICAL
6 TERRACE
7 KITCHEN
8 BEDROOM
9 GARAGE

MAIN FLOOR PLAN

1 ENTRY
2 COURTYARD
3 LOGGIA
4 RECEPTION ROOM
5 BEDROOM
6 LIBRARY
7 LIVING ROOM
8 DINING
9 KITCHEN
10 SITTING ROOM
11 TERRACE
12 MASTER SUITE
13 POOL

# La Toscana

*Kirk B. and*

*Genevieve Johnson House*

Above: Terrace. Opposite: Hall

## IN THE 1920S MR. AND MRS. KIRK JOHNSON SET OUT TO BUILD THEIR OWN

version of a Tuscan villa in Montecito, California, just east of Santa Barbara. They selected a twelve-acre site with an 1880s farmhouse (subsequently razed) set among indigenous live oaks and shrubs and Monterey cypresses of considerable age. For the architect of La Toscana (now known as Sotto al Monte) they chose George Washington Smith, who had built a national reputation designing Spanish-style houses in the Santa Barbara area. He brought in Los Angeles landscape architect A. E. Hanson, with whom he had previously worked. The house was completed in 1928; the gardens, in 1929.

Smith loosely based La Toscana's design on the seventeenth-century Villa Gamberaia, drawing upon its extreme simplicity, its rectangular form, the detailing of its entrance surround, windows, and quoins, and the axial connection between house and garden. The villa may have been on the Italian tour Smith took with his wife and the Johnsons in 1927,[1] and it was also familiar by reproduction in Edith Wharton's *Italian Villas and Their Gardens* (1904), illustrated by Maxfield Parrish (see fig. 1 in Introduction).

Parrish's popular images captured dreamlike vistas of Italy—which certainly paralleled the features of the Johnson estate. Hanson described the view from the house north toward the Santa Ynez Mountains as

> *the very essence of Montecito: there were beautiful native oaks in the foreground, framing the view of the mountains, which were, due to the distance, a light, bluish-grey—a fine contrast with the dark green oaks in the immediate foreground. It was like a Maxfield Parrish painting.*[2]

Opposite: Cortile. Above: Library. Overleaf: Pergola

Smith's own aesthetic preferences, which leaned toward the Spanish and Italian Primitive painters,[3] are reflected in the overall simplicity and rusticity of the exterior. Deep, overhanging hipped roofs covered with dark brown terra-cotta tile shade the buff-colored stucco walls. Stone arcades, quoins, and other details were sandblasted to produce a weathered texture. Wooden shutters, originally painted ultramarine blue, and wrought-iron grilles further ornament the house.

The interior strikes a balance between comfort and refinement. A loggia (now glazed) and terrace provided easy outdoor access, while the interior is notable for its elegant elements, including the formal entrance hall, curved staircase, highly polished Monte Verde stone columns, and elaborate beamed and coffered ceilings. At the south end of the groin-vaulted hallway are the drawing room, the library, and a doorway that opens to a double staircase and the English lawn beyond. The north end of the hall divides, leading to the dining room and a suite of bedrooms. Locating the principal bedrooms on the first floor was an informality that broke from traditional plans for a house of this type and scale. Additional bedrooms for guests and staff were on the second floor.

Outside, Hanson created a remarkably diverse landscape, similar in effect to Wharton's description of Villa Gamberaia's gardens, with "free circulation of sunlight and air about the house; abundance of water; easy access to dense shade; sheltered walks with different points of view; variety of effect produced by the skillful use of different levels; and finally, breadth and simplicity of composition."[4]

Hanson's landscape, like Villa Gamberaia's, featured distinct spaces, each with its own character: a gently sloping lawn (which now includes a pool and cabana) that trails into the woods, balustraded terraces stepping down to ornamental gardens with clipped hedges, and a simple gravel entrance court with a fountain, reached by a drive lined with pittosporum to create a "green tunnel."[5] The formal entrance is flanked by a pair of Monterey cypress, and the terrace to the east contains a fifteenth-century well head and a large dragon tree. Level ground east of the terrace was limited, and Hanson filled it with a simple parterre of clipped boxwood.[6]

The terrace or "cortile" off the dining room leads to a westward path flanked by terra-cotta pots of small orange trees. The path's gentle incline terminates at a fountain, which is surrounded by circular paving laid with black and white pebbles. The formality of this axial path—which is analogous to one at Villa Gamberaia—contrasts with the naturalistic planting of the surrounding oaks. Elsewhere are small landscape vignettes, such as vine-covered pergolas and quiet corners adorned with sculpture. Altogether, La Toscana's magical outdoor "rooms" recall Wharton's praise of their predecessors.

> [T]he real value of the old Italian garden-plan is that logic and beauty meet in it, as they should in all sound architectural work. Each quarter of the garden was placed where convenience required, and was made accessible from all the others by the most direct and rational means; and from this intelligent method of planning the most varying effects of unexpectedness and beauty were obtained.[7]

1. Robert Nathan Cram, "The Important Italian Villas: A Brief Guide," *House Beautiful*, June 1926, 814; Patricia Gebhard, 136.

2. Hanson, 73.

3. John Taylor Boyd, "Houses Showing A Distinguished Simplicity," *Arts & Decoration* 33 (October 1930), 57.

4. Wharton, 46. The garden at Villa Gamberaia was also the precedent for one of Charles Platt's most published estates, Faulkner Farm, in Brookline, Massachusetts (1897–98). Morgan, "Al Fresco: An Overview of Charles A. Platt's *Italian Gardens*," in Platt, 128.

5. Hanson, 73.

6. Streatfield, 130.

7. Wharton, 47.

Above: Garden view. Below: Dining room

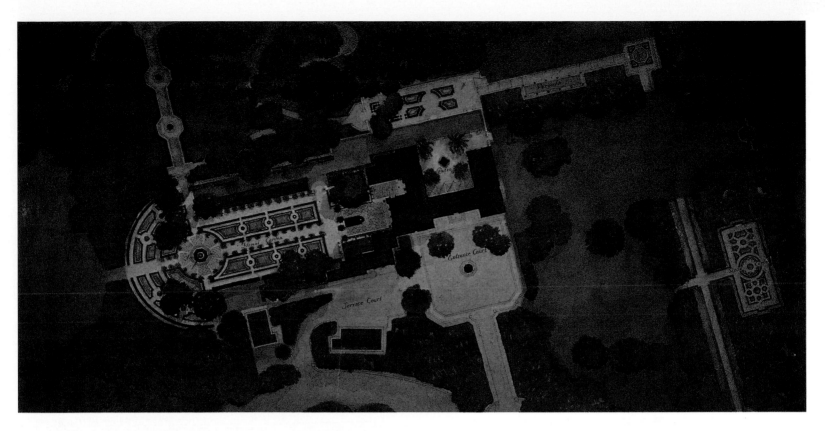

Above: A. E. Hanson. Site plan for La Toscana, 1928–29. Archibald E. Hanson Collection, Architecture & Design Collection, University Art Museum, University of California Santa Barbara. Below left: Staircase

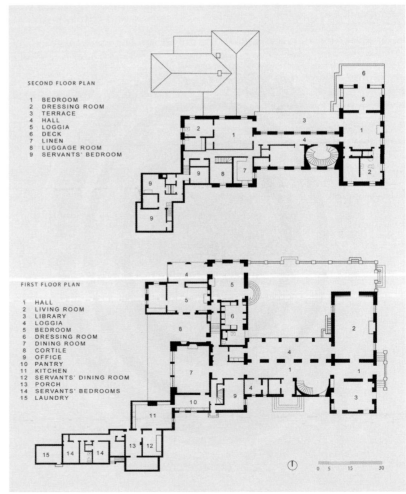

SECOND FLOOR PLAN

1  BEDROOM
2  DRESSING ROOM
3  TERRACE
4  HALL
5  LOGGIA
6  DECK
7  LINEN
8  LUGGAGE ROOM
9  SERVANTS' BEDROOM

FIRST FLOOR PLAN

1  HALL
2  LIVING ROOM
3  LIBRARY
4  LOGGIA
5  BEDROOM
6  DRESSING ROOM
7  DINING ROOM
8  CORTILE
9  OFFICE
10  PANTRY
11  KITCHEN
12  SERVANTS' DINING ROOM
13  PORCH
14  SERVANTS' BEDROOMS
15  LAUNDRY

0    5    15    30

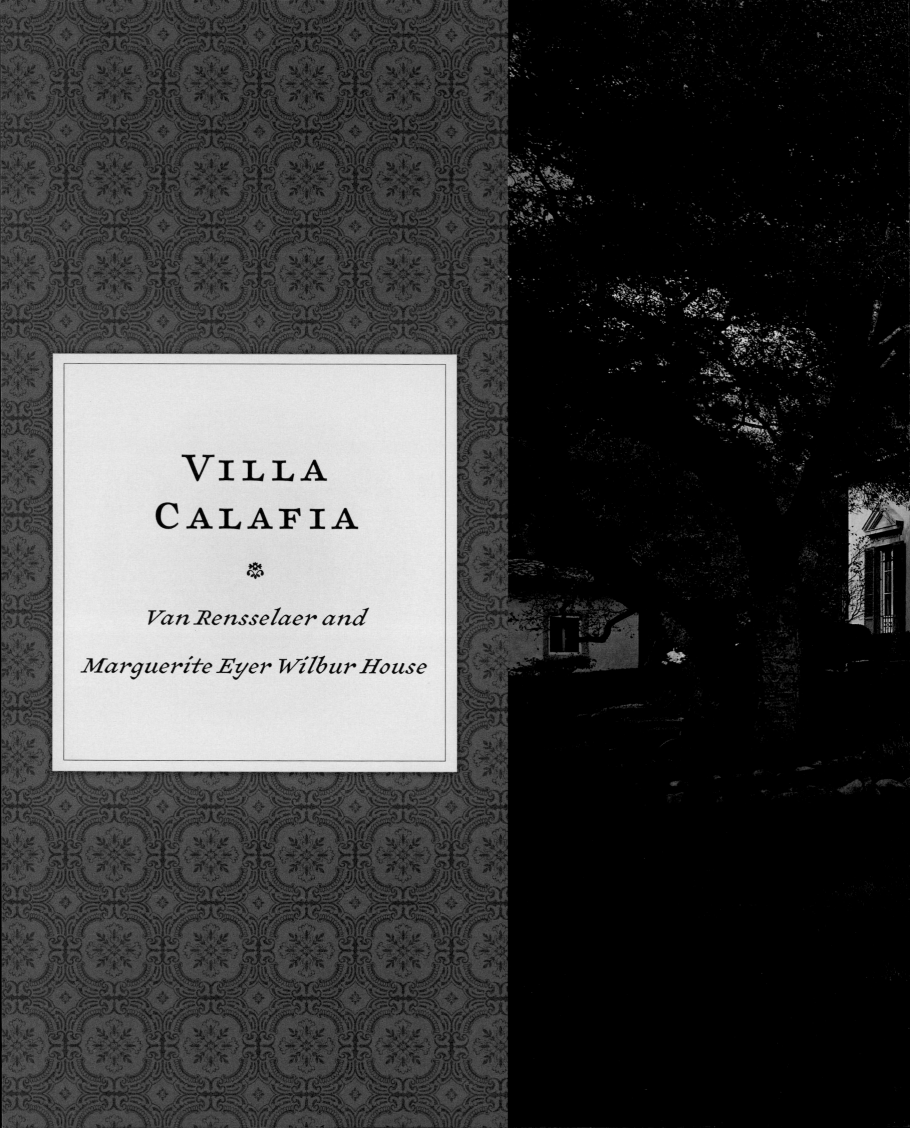

# VILLA
# CALAFIA

❧

*Van Rensselaer and*

*Marguerite Eyer Wilbur House*

Above: Entrance gate. Opposite: Main guesthouse

## VILLA CALAFIA, IN CALIFORNIA'S SANTA BARBARA COUNTY, LIES IN A CANYON

north of the Pacific Ocean (the coastline in this area runs east to west). Two creeks course through the roughly triangular property, which is densely planted with native coastal oaks and exotic trees. The villa, constructed in 1932–35 (with later additions), was designed by Los Angeles architect Gordon B. Kaufmann for Van Rensselaer and Marguerite Eyer Wilbur,[1] Pasadenans who sought to establish a second home in the Santa Barbara area.

Apparently the Wilburs never built a principal residence on the site. Instead, an ensemble of buildings was constructed: a main guesthouse, which serves as the principal residence; a smaller guesthouse, used today as an art gallery; a garage/service quarters organized around a courtyard; and a gardener's house. A meandering gravel driveway separates the service buildings from the guesthouses. The main guesthouse ("guesthouse no. 1" on the site plan) is roughly at the center of the property, with a terrace and garden following the downward-sloping contour of the land behind it. To the west and across a creek is the second guesthouse. A barn, lathhouse, and terrace are the other structures on the estate.

Kaufmann borrowed the severely simple form of the Tuscan farmhouse for Villa Calafia and connected the buildings to the landscaped setting with terraces. In contrast to contemporaneous Mediterranean-style houses that merely imitated the surface ornament or distinctive roof profiles of the past, Villa Calafia appears to have a genuine connection with such forebears as Villa Gamberaia and other Italian Renaissance villas. Kauffman provided a hint of his approach to the Mediterranean architectural vocabulary in an article on another residence he designed, the Eisner house in Beverly Hills (1925).

Above: Main guesthouse, loggia. Opposite: Main guesthouse, entry

*The exterior walls of white stucco—the only possible treatment for such a house—provide a background to the play of light and shadow from the . . . trees and shrubs. . . . Underneath the jutting edge of the roof of tile—which wards off the heat of the sun besides forming an attractive color contrast—are small windows such as are characteristic of all Mediterranean houses that look out over the blue of the Cote d'Azur along that famous coast in Southern France or the Italian Riviera. . . . No attempt was made to "drag in" a picturesque detail.[2]*

The main guesthouse at Villa Calafia incorporates other architectural elements that were part of a design repertoire Kaufmann derived from historical precedents, including a second-story open loggia. This functions as an elegant update of the sleeping porch, which had enjoyed prominence during the earlier Arts and Crafts period,[3] and links the upper floor to the surrounding environment. Another of Kaufmann's favorite features was the groin vault, which he introduced in the entrance hallway, where it adds sculptural interest yet maintains the simplicity of the solid white walls. (Originally this space was open

Above: Main guesthouse, living room. Below: Main guesthouse, family room

at both ends, functioning as a breezeway.) Other sculptural elements Kaufmann frequently deployed include corner fireplaces and carved or deeply coffered ceilings, both of which appear in the living room.

The current owners have sensitively added to the original structures. A new kitchen and family room in the main guesthouse provide handsome, much needed spaces to what was planned as a temporary residence. Collectors of contemporary art, they have converted the second guesthouse into a gallery. Old columns were brought to the rear of the building, taking root among the sandstone boulders naturally strewn there.

1. Marguerite Wilbur was an authority on California history who wrote several books, including *Immortal Pirate: The Life of Sir Francis Drake* (New York: Hastings House, 1951), and translated many others, including Alexandre Dumas's *A Gil Blas in California* (Los Angeles: The Primavera Press, 1933).

2. Gordon B. Kaufmann, "A House of Tuscan Inspiration," *Arts & Decoration* 28:4 (February 1928), 95.

3. Jan Furey Muntz, "Gordon B. Kaufmann: California Classicism," in Jay Belloli, ed., *Johnson, Kaufmann, Coate: Partners in the California Style* (Claremont, Calif.: Trustees of Scripps College, 1992), 31.

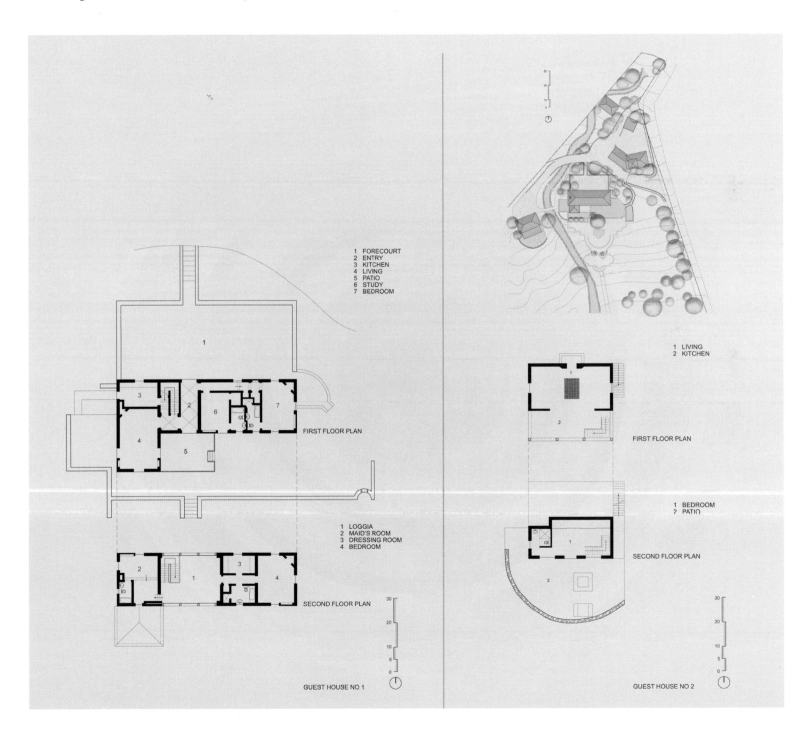

1 FORECOURT
2 ENTRY
3 KITCHEN
4 LIVING
5 PATIO
6 STUDY
7 BEDROOM

FIRST FLOOR PLAN

1 LOGGIA
2 MAID'S ROOM
3 DRESSING ROOM
4 BEDROOM

SECOND FLOOR PLAN

GUEST HOUSE NO 1

1 LIVING
2 KITCHEN

FIRST FLOOR PLAN

1 BEDROOM
2 PATIO

SECOND FLOOR PLAN

GUEST HOUSE NO 2

# PLAZA
# RUBIO
# HOUSES

Above: Street view. Opposite: View from entry toward Mission Santa Barbara

IN THE SHADOW OF SANTA BARBARA'S HISTORIC FRANCISCAN MISSION
is a small residential enclave along the Plaza Rubio, which was built as part of new tract laid out in 1925. The street was named for Father José González Rubio, the last of the Mission's Franciscan administrators, who was buried there in 1875. The tract includes a *paseo*, or interior street, that bisects the block and extends south to East Padre Street.

Most of the houses that line Plaza Rubio were commissioned by Margaret Knight Andrews, who had purchased seven of the eight lots fronting the mission in 1924. Andrews was active in Santa Barbara's planning organizations, whose work took on urgency after a devastating earthquake in 1925. Her decision to develop the row of houses in a Spanish or Mediterranean style—sympathetic in design to the mission—may have been influenced by the earlier recommendations of city planner Charles Mulford Robinson to unify Santa Barbara's image with architecture drawn from its Spanish colonial past. Andrews also developed a number of commercial properties locally, all in the Spanish or Mediterranean mode.

Andrews hired Mary McLaughlin Craig to design seven Plaza Rubio houses, six opposite the mission and the seventh around the corner at Laguna and East Padre Streets. (414 Plaza Rubio was designed by P. W. Noble, a local builder.) Craig was the widow of James Osborne Craig, a Scottish architect who had designed El Paseo, one of the early, pre-earthquake buildings that helped establish a Mediterranean direction for the city's downtown architecture.[1] While not a trained architect, she was a gifted designer, and she conceived the Plaza Rubio houses in relation to one another as well as to the mission. Of the local movement to promote new design in the context of existing buildings Craig wrote, "in architecture as in

Left: Patio. Above: Lockwood DeForest. Millicent Estabrook Garden for 408 Plaza Rubio. 1936. Smithsonian Institution, Washington, D.C., Archives of American Gardens, Garden Club of America Collection. Opposite top: Dining room. Opposite bottom: Street view

literature, the underlying trend of old association, not tacked onto the fabric but woven into it, has a charm that nothing else can give."[2]

The Plaza Rubio houses share a set of identifiable Mediterranean features: white or light-colored stucco walls, low-pitched tile roofs, and interiors whose lightly painted plaster walls contrast with dark hardwood floors and exposed ceiling beams. Consistent with the Mediterranean tradition of site planning, the houses are set close to the front property line, reserving most of the outdoor space for the more private rear areas of the lots. The footprint of each two-story house incorporates setbacks for courtyards and patios. Craig ingeniously sited the houses so that they visually share open space with the neighboring lots. Additionally, patios, terraces, or courtyards significantly extend the living space to the outdoors. The interiors are moderate in size, but the occasional use of double-height rooms or entire walls that open to the outdoors dramatically expands the sense of space. Elsewhere Craig incorporated views of the mission, large sculptural fireplaces, and second-floor casement windows with views of sloping tile roofs, which likewise lend spaciousness to the modest dwellings.

In contrast with the other houses, 408 Plaza Rubio was conceived for a double lot, creating a usable side yard/driveway, and its entrance

faces southwest (the others look northwest, toward the mission). The house was designed for Andrews's sister Elizabeth Knight.[3] A garden by well-known local landscape architect Lockwood DeForest filled the lot to the east of the house; in recent years, the garden was replaced by a house.

The partnership of Margaret Andrews and Mary Craig uniquely and lastingly contributed to Santa Barbara's development. At a time when the city was just beginning to formulate its ideas about unifying its commercial buildings with a Mediterranean design, this female team of developer and designer were pioneers in applying the concept to an ensemble of efficient, ingeniously designed residences.

1. E-mail from Mary Louise Days to author, April 28, 2007.

2. Mrs. James Osborne Craig, "The Heritage of All California," *California Southland* 33 (September 1922), 8. Pamela Skewes-Cox, Mary Craig's granddaughter, provided this reference.

3. Architect George Washington Smith may have been consulted in the design of the house, based on documentary evidence in Smith's office records owned by the Architecture and Design Collection, University of California Santa Barbara. Mary Louise Days, "City Landmark Designation of Portions of Plaza Rubio Tract and Its Environs," Council Agenda Report, City of Santa Barbara, September 11, 1992, 4.

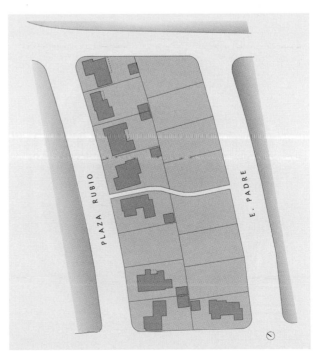

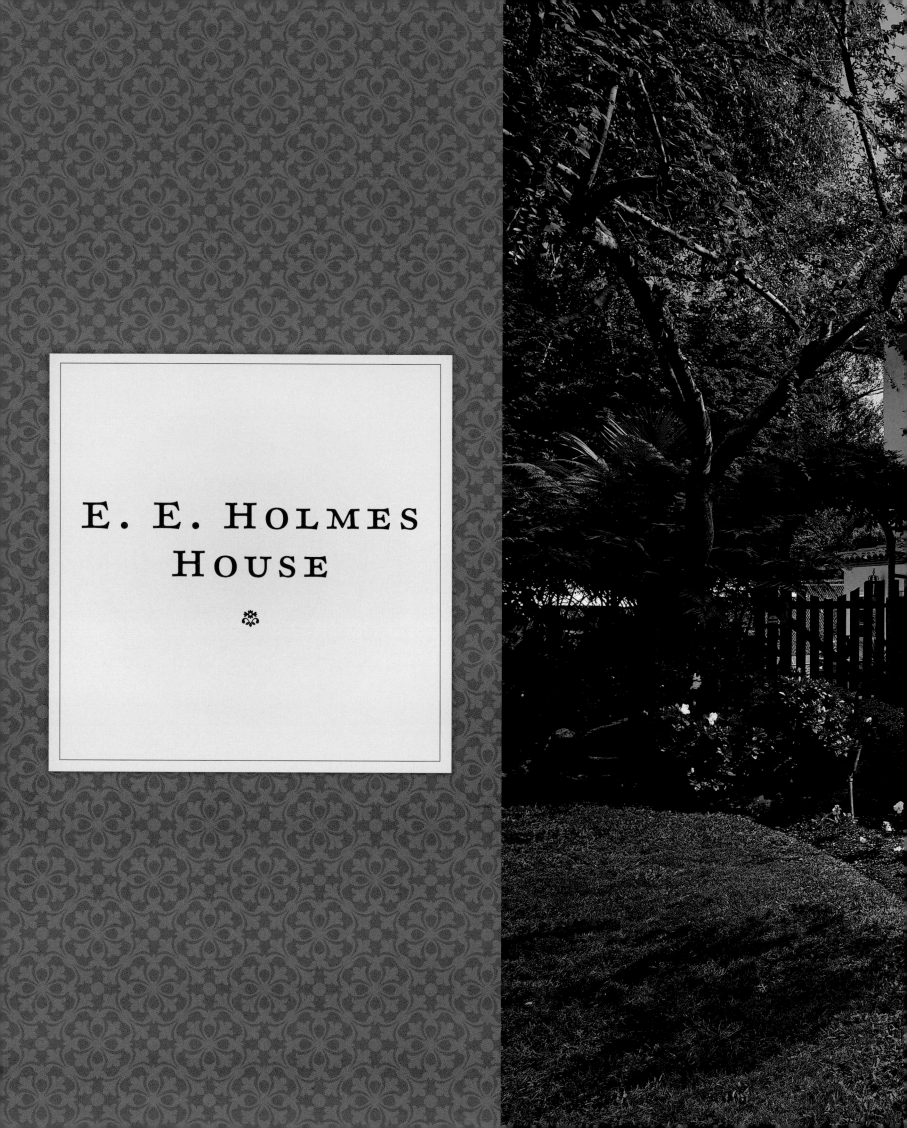

# E. E. HOLMES
# HOUSE

❖

Above: Terrace. Opposite: Enclosed terrace (now family room)

ONE OF THE UNITED STATES' FEW PLANNED COMMUNITIES TO BE UNIFIED
around the style of Mediterranean architecture and landscape is California's Rancho Palos Verdes. Southwest of Los Angeles,
between the city of Redondo Beach and the Los Angeles Harbor, Palos Verdes boasts a magnificent site and a community plan
that closely coordinated landscape architecture, urban design, and architecture.

Following earlier unsuccessful attempts to develop the site, the Olmsted Brothers landscape architecture firm, city planner
Charles Cheney, and architect Myron Hunt began plans for Palos Verdes' thirty-two hundred acres in 1923. Eight hundred
acres, including four miles of shoreline, were set aside for a golf course, a swimming pool, and open parkland, some of which
was planted with trees, shrubs, and flowers. The vast majority of the remaining land was set aside for single-family residences.
Four commercial centers were proposed, though only one, Malaga Cove Plaza, was constructed. To ensure high architectural
standards, a design review committee called the Art Jury was established. Restrictions addressed architectural types, roof con-
figurations, and minimum building costs. While no specific image was mandated, historic photographs as well as views of Palos
Verdes today reveal a strong commitment to the Mediterranean tradition.

Many of Los Angeles's leading architects were commissioned to design houses in Palos Verdes, among them H. Roy Kelley,
a gifted young designer who garnered numerous awards for his residential work.[1] One of his projects was a Spanish Revival
house for E. E. Holmes, completed in 1929. While subsequent owners have expanded the property with a second lot, enlarged

the house, and augmented the landscape with new terraces and water features, the original design's simplicity—with solid, off-white stucco walls and low-pitched hipped roofs—remains intact.

The house is sited at virtually the center of a southwest-sloping lot, with expansive views of the Pacific Ocean. By placing the house back from the road, Kelley made the entrance "which is really the rear of the house, . . . sheltered and partly enclosed, offering privacy for the garden and creating the feeling of a small estate."[2]

Using space economically and taking full advantage of the view were Kelley's prevailing concerns. As originally designed, the circulation in the one-and-one-half-story house pivoted around a tight, curved entrance hall. The hall separated the living room from the service wing on the first floor and accommodated the staircase to the second floor. The spacious double-height living room with exposed beams opened to a small library and a terrace with an outdoor fireplace. Originally the terrace was sheltered by a pergola covered with peeled branches and vines; today it is enclosed by a glass roof, which allows muted light to bathe the space. The adjacent dining room offered a full view of the ocean. Three bedrooms were located on the second floor.

Kelley credited his clients for having "helped me in planning the house by giving me a complete word picture of their ideas. Owing to their fine taste and appreciation, working with them was most enjoyable."[3] The result of their collaboration was a house of simplicity and restraint. Kelley carefully composed the house's large, plain masses,

placing the few openings where function dictated and adding interest with unfussy details: a tile roof, wrought-iron pot holders, wooden shutters, and the pergola. It is a house for Everyman, devoid of pretense or exoticism.

Kelley made his views on the value of understatement clear in "Simplicity Is the Keynote of Beauty," one of the most important essays on the subject published in the 1920s. Kelley saw the public's growing appreciation of architectural simplicity as an indication of increased sophistication. Writing in October 1929, at the onset of the Great Depression, he also acknowledged the economic as well as

aesthetic benefits of simplicity, suggesting that if costs are contained by "simplicity of form and detail rather than the use of poor materials and construction [and we] dispense with some of the needless ornamental features, then we will produce homes that will never be 'out-of-date.' "[4] The Holmes house's original cost barely exceeded the minimum of $10,000 mandated for this portion of Palos Verdes.

In addition to his custom-designed houses Kelley designed a group of nine speculative houses in Palos Verdes, of which six were built. They were priced from $3,500 to $4,500 and located in an area with a minimum construction cost of $3,500. In a somewhat defensive tone,

Below: Living room. Opposite: Library

Above: Archival view of garden terrace. c. 1931. Courtesy of the Palos Verdes (Calif.) Library District, Local History Collection. Below: Rear facade (former garden terrace)

the local paper cited the houses as evidence that Palos Verdes was not only for the wealthy: "It brings to the man and woman of moderate means the same participation, if they will, in the increasingly rich community life, the library, the clubs, and the prestige, already considerable, of living in a community known nationally for its high ideals and its successful planning."[5]

1. "Los Angeles Architects Win National Prizes," *Los Angeles Times*, August 4, 1929, D1.

2. "A Home in Palos Verdes," *Sunset* 66:2 (February 1931), 28.

3. Ibid.

4. H. Roy Kelley, "Simplicity Is the Keynote of Beauty," *California Arts and Architecture* 36 (October 1929), 38.

5. "Palos Verdes Has Property of All Kinds," *Palos Verdes Bulletin* 5:11 (November 1929), 3.

H. Roy Kelley. Speculative house for Palos Verdes, California. Archival view. c. 1929.
Courtesy of the Palos Verdes Library District, Local History Collection

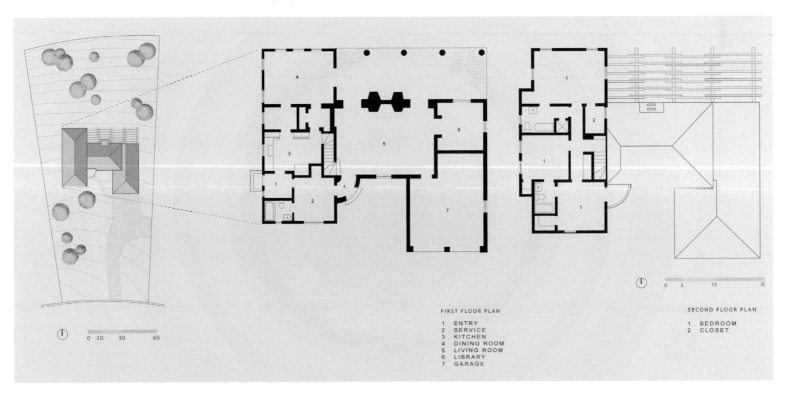

FIRST FLOOR PLAN

1 ENTRY
2 SERVICE
3 KITCHEN
4 DINING ROOM
5 LIVING ROOM
6 LIBRARY
7 GARAGE

SECOND FLOOR PLAN

1 BEDROOM
2 CLOSET

# STEVENS-
# HUGHES
# HOUSE

Above: Eastern courtyard. Opposite: Living room. Overleaf: Library

## THE DESIGN OF THE STATELY STEVENS-HUGHES HOUSE (1927–29)

is a response to its physical context. The house sits on a prominent corner, stretched over three city lots, in one of the oldest sections of Coral Gables, Florida, a community inspired by the Mediterranean and the popular 1920s image of "castles in Spain." It is also directly across the street from the city's first golf course (1922), part of the system of landscaped open spaces and recreational areas that was central to the overall concept and development of Coral Gables.

Charles Phelps Stevens and Jennie Stevens, residents of Albany, New York, commissioned architect Dudley St. Clair Donnelly to design the house.[1] Donnelly himself was new to the area, having recently arrived from New London, Connecticut, where he had designed a wide range of buildings.[2] Donnelly's design has a castlelike quality: The central two-story mass has a romantic balcony above a recessed entrance porch and is framed by one-story extensions; the second-story roof has a stepped parapet and corner towers. (An attached garage is a clear reminder that it is in fact a twentieth-century house.) The roof was originally covered by old Cuban tile, a dictate of the community's founder, George Merrick, meant to add instantly a patina of age to Coral Gables. The existing terra-cotta tiles may not be original but their dark red color contrasts strikingly with the pale stucco (over concrete block) walls.

In the H-plan house, Donnelly created a series of contrasts between intimate, enclosed spaces and others that flow easily into the outdoors. The living room, in the center of the plan, has an open, airy quality, due, in part, to its wide proportions and coolly elegant use of picket-shaped floor tiles. Additionally, triple-hung windows visually connect to the adjacent courtyards. An

arcaded porch provides a transition to the intimate western courtyard, home to caged exotic birds. The larger eastern courtyard is cooled by a wall fountain flowing into a Japanese koi pond. Other typically Mediterranean features of this courtyard are the richly colored decorative tiles and the pair of wrought-iron grilles built into a wall to provide views of a side garden. The eastern courtyard connects to the family room via a French door flanked by windows.

The more enclosed spaces include the stair hall (to the right of the entry), with a staircase adorned by wrought-iron railings made by noted Philadelphia metal designer Samuel Yellin. To the left is a tiny but sumptuous library, which was remodeled in 1929 by architect Phineas Paist

for the Hughes family. (The original owner, Charles Stevens, had died a mere seven months after the house's completion.[3]) This cozy room has a large stone fireplace in the corner and linen-fold paneling. The ground floor also has two bedrooms and baths; the house was designed to function comfortably on one level, although two additional bedroom suites, linked by an arcaded balcony, were provided on the second floor.

The landscaping has gone through a series of changes owing to repeated hurricanes and a desire to use the rear of the house fully. Today a wide pergola provides a transition from the ground floor to a large pool and a cabana at the back of the property. Palm trees are planted along the perimeter.

As one of the residences within the Country Club of Coral Gables Historic District, the Stevens-Hughes house serves as an exemplar of the excellent design and landscaping that fostered the development of a community with architectural integrity and longevity.

1. Working drawings on file at the Building and Zoning Department, Coral Gables, Florida.

2. "Prominent Architect Occupies Office in Chaplin Building," *Miami Riviera of Coral Gables*, vol. 21 (June 4, 1926), 1. He may have been attracted to Coral Gables by the construction of the new Biltmore Hotel and Country Club; he was involved with the construction of the Belleview Country Club in Clearwater, Florida, owned by the Biltmore-Bowman Corporation.

3. "Charles Phelps Stevens," *Miami Daily News and Metropolis*, December 22, 1927.

Opposite: Pool view. Above: Balcony over eastern courtyard

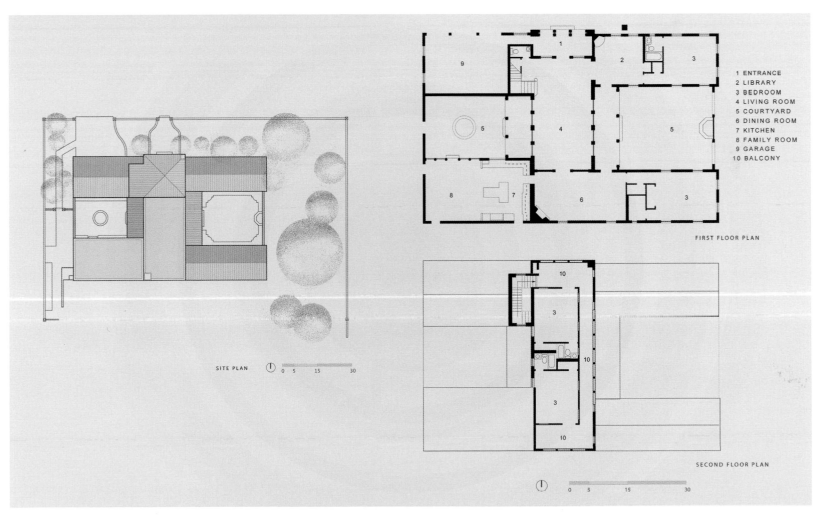

SITE PLAN  0 5 15 30

1 ENTRANCE
2 LIBRARY
3 BEDROOM
4 LIVING ROOM
5 COURTYARD
6 DINING ROOM
7 KITCHEN
8 FAMILY ROOM
9 GARAGE
10 BALCONY

FIRST FLOOR PLAN

SECOND FLOOR PLAN

0 5 15 30

# HERBERT LEE
## *and* ELIZABETH
## KOKERNOT
## HOUSE

Above: Reception hall. Opposite: Reception hall, view to living room

## THE MONTE VISTA NEIGHBORHOOD IN SAN ANTONIO, TEXAS,

is a well-designed, remarkably intact residential enclave where Mediterranean houses figure prominently. It encompasses nearly one hundred city blocks stretched across a rocky hill north of the central business district. Monte Vista was recognized as a historic district by San Antonio in 1975 and listed in the National Register of Historic Places in 1998. According to the National Register nomination,

> The neighborhood developed slowly between 1882 and the turn of the century before booming in the 1920s and 1930s. As a result, architect designed period revival residences coexist with more modest vernacular dwellings, bungalows and apartment houses lining the neighborhood's streets. Enlivening the basic rectilinear grid, its boulevards and parkways feature distinctive landscaping elements such as entry gates and rows of street trees.[1]

Monte Vista was promoted as a "high-class subdivision,"[2] where "the superb skills of Nature and ingenious minds of men have joined forces in making [it] one of the most delightful residential parks in the South."[3] The development company, Rogers-Hill, invested heavily in street improvements and installation of utility lines. It also imposed building restrictions, setting minimums for lot sizes and building costs, prohibited commercial development, and allowed only Caucasians to purchase houses.

Herbert Lee Kokernot, a rancher who was president of the San Antonio Development Company, which sold the land to Rogers-Hill, built two substantial houses in Monte Vista, noting, "The fact that I own property in Monte Vista is suf-

ficient evidence of my complete faith in it."[4] Kokernot came from a distinguished family of Texas cattle barons and landowners. When he and his wife, Elizabeth, moved to San Antonio in 1907, their holdings included vast spreads in Brewster, Jeff Davis, and Pecos counties. Kokernot became a key figure in statewide ranching issues, holding leadership positions in a number of related organizations.[5]

The Kokernots' first house in Monte Vista was a fourteen-room "mansion which has long been considered one of San Antonio's most beautiful residences."[6] By 1928 the Kokernots wanted to downsize and commissioned the Russell Brown Company to design a new house—which, at 102 feet by 71 feet, was hardly diminutive. Brown was originally from California, and he had established a substantial architectural practice in Houston before beginning his projects in San Antonio.[7]

From the street the Spanish Revival Kokernot house has an extremely formal appearance, which reflected the Kokernots' social standing as distinguished business leaders and philanthropists. A pair

Above: Bedroom. Opposite: Library. Overleaf: Retreat

of enormous, abundant oaks partially screens the house, softening the effect. The front door is framed by Spanish-style Solomonic corkscrew columns with massive finials and scrolling. The walls on either side step back, emphasizing the front door's imposing character. Symmetrically positioned French doors with wrought-iron balconies and windows with cast-stone details provide additional visual interest to the facade, as does a balustrade enclosing a shallow terrace that extends across its full length. The stucco walls (laid over hollow clay tile) are painted a faint pink, which changes hue throughout the day depending on the sun and shadows. The roof is covered in terra-cotta tiles. Characteristic of houses in Monte Vista, the garage is at the rear of the property; a porte cochere at the west side provides access to the driveway and garage. To the east, an enclosed porch echoes the shape of the porte cochere.

Past the front door is a grand reception hall, detailed with cast-stone engaged piers, brackets, and surface ornaments, as well as groin vaults above the doorways to the living room and library. In contrast to the reception hall, those rooms have an intimate quality, with large fireplaces as their focal points. The reception hall also is distinguished by a pair of staircases. Between the stairs, wrought-iron gates open to the dining room, whose bowed far wall terminates the flow of movement that began at the entrance.

The double staircase turns, before reaching the second floor, at a landing that opens into a retreat (perhaps a conservatory originally). The floor of this handsome room is covered with patterned green Redondo tiles from Mexico. (They are made by a technique wherein colored pigment and marble dust are poured into molds overlaid on

Portland cement. The tiles are hydraulically pressed to increase density and strength, then cured under water for twenty-four hours for additional durability.[8]) Above is an exposed-beam ceiling, and at the end of the room stands a fireplace.

The house forms an irregularly shaped T, with the central segment separating the rear of the property into a garden and a service space. The latter includes the garage, tool room, gardening room, and servants' quarters. From the house, the principal access to the garden is through a loggia, built later. The garden's leading feature is a large, organically shaped pool and poolside fountains constructed in 1948. The pool is surrounded by a lush lawn. Bathhouses are at the back of the garden; dense foliage provides a natural edge around the outdoor space.

The Kokernot house is one of the finest Mediterranean houses in Monte Vista and an outstanding example of the high-quality design,

materials, and craftsmanship that contribute to the neighborhood's historic significance.

1. Pfeiffer and Pemberton-Haugh.

2. *San Antonio Express*, May 17, 1925, as quoted in the National Register nomination.

3. As quoted by Everett, 29.

4. Ibid., 30.

5. Herbert Lee Kokernot was president of the Cattle Raisers' Association of Texas (now the Texas and Southwestern Cattle Raisers Association), president of the Alpine-Marfa Highland Hereford Association, and president and cofounder of the Texas Livestock Marketing Association. "Herbert Lee Kokernot," The Handbook of Texas Online, tsha.utexas.edu/handbook/online/articles/KK/fko3.html, May 4, 2007.

6. Everett, 83.

7. See Fox, *Spanish-Mediterranean Houses of Houston*, 26.

8. Brochure, Redondo Tile Collection, San Antonio, c. 2006.

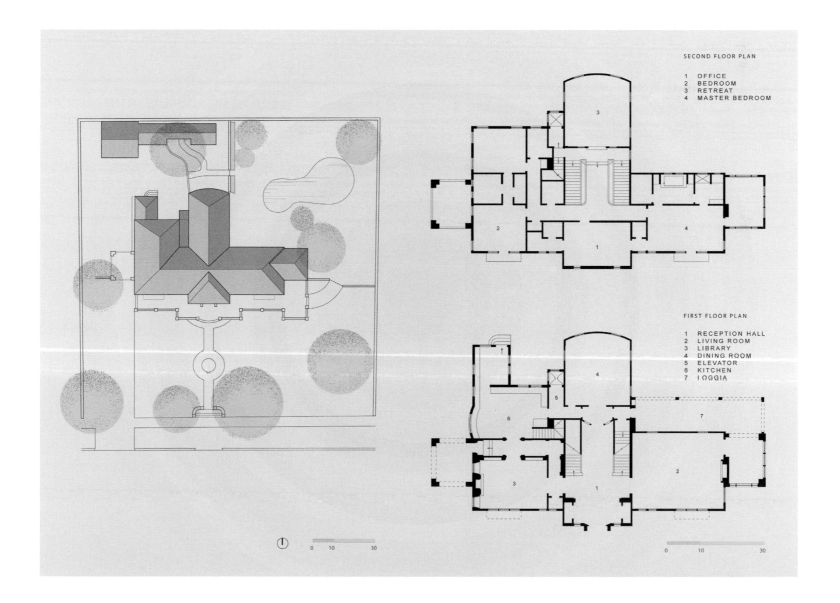

SECOND FLOOR PLAN

1 OFFICE
2 BEDROOM
3 RETREAT
4 MASTER BEDROOM

FIRST FLOOR PLAN

1 RECEPTION HALL
2 LIVING ROOM
3 LIBRARY
4 DINING ROOM
5 ELEVATOR
6 KITCHEN
7 LOGGIA

# PERCY L. MANNEN HOUSE

Side view, from driveway

## Oakmont was, like Monte Vista, a residential neighborhood

in San Antonio, Texas, with elevated social aspirations. (Today it is considered part of the larger Monte Vista district.) Promotional literature of the 1920s described Oakmont atmospherically: "A quiet exclusion of all that is ordinary establishes a background for that individuality and personality which the smart world demands of its leaders."[1] The site was characterized as a "lovely woodland [separated] from the drumming arteries of trade. Pervaded by an atmosphere of unmarred serenity, Oakmont lies high above the city, coolly aloof like a fine old English park, its gentle knolls graciously inviting."[2]

Thomas Masterson, a former state representative and senator, had engaged the W. L. Coleman Company to develop and market Oakmont in the early 1920s[3] and was the first to build a home there. Another resident was Percy L. Mannen, a successful sales agent and/or manager at the National Cash Register Company in San Antonio.[4] Mannen's 1927 house is among the finest examples of the residential work by the prominent San Antonio firm Ayres and Ayres, father-and-son architects who specialized in the Mediterranean Revival style and designed a number of houses in the district. Mannen may have selected Ayres and Ayres because it had designed the nearby Thomas E. Hogg House (1923), considered the firm's first major success in the design of a Spanish house.

Located on the crest of a sloping site, the Mannen house has an imposing presence, though it lacks the formality of the nearby Kokernot house. Instead, Ayres and Ayres created a residence whose simplicity of form, materials, and details reflects both vernacular Mexican styles (as transplanted to California) and the Andalusian farmhouse.[5] Atlee Ayres (the father) had visited Spain in 1921 and during a 1923 trip to Los Angeles was enthralled by the Spanish Revival houses he saw and photographed. During the latter trip he met with well-known practitioners of the Spanish Colonial style and identified craftsmen and manufacturers of decorative elements for his projects. He even wrote a book, *Mexican Architecture: Domestic, Civil & Ecclesiastical* (1926), demonstrating the depth of his interest in and knowledge of the subject.

Ayres's biographer, Robert James Coote, suggested that the Spanish style appealed to him because he realized, after designing houses in the Italian vein, that

> *In scale and character, in construction and craftsmanship, the authentic Italian model was not suitable for contemporary houses in San Antonio. . . . Soon he began to look more to a corollary prototype of more manageable scale, less demanding composition, less strict vocabulary or ornament, and more related to San Antonio's past and present character, landscape and climate.[6]*

At the Hogg and Mannen houses, and at several other important projects, Ayres used a similar approach to siting. He located the entrance within a two-story volume, then pivoted the balance of the plan at a forty-five-degree angle to capture the prevailing southwestern breezes. This device, one of several ways Ayres passively cooled his buildings, also served an aesthetic purpose, breaking up the mass of the house into a series of simple, abstract volumes that interact with the landscape.

At the Mannen house, many features address such practical and aesthetic goals simultaneously, including the numerous openings to the outdoors. A pair of wrought-iron and glass windows looked out from the dining room to the front lawn. (These unfortunately were converted to fixed glass.) A second-story balcony with carved wooden columns and railings cantilevers over these windows. Originally, a single-bay pergola covered with peeled bark logs (later replaced by a larger paved patio) extended beyond the entrance facade toward a side porch. In the living room, in the one-story space to the left of the entrance, three large, arched glass and iron French doors opened to a loggia with deep, arched openings; one set survives, and two have been replaced with windows. The shaded extension cooled the living room, as the cantilevered balcony did the dining room. Each of the three

Archival view. c. 1927. Courtesy of the Atlee B. Ayres Collection, Institute of Texan Cultures, University of Texas San Antonio. No. 105-0700

bedrooms upstairs (now somewhat reconfigured) originally had direct access to the outdoors through the front balcony or sleeping porches, creating cool, comfortable accommodations.

Other exterior features demonstrate Ayres's interest in the Spanish style. To simulate thick, handmade walls, he applied stucco in a slightly irregular pattern to walls of hollow terra-cotta brick and rounded the edges of the walls. Large terra-cotta tiles cover the roof planes. Ayres went to pains to get the right glazed tile for the frame surrounding the entrance and the wall fountain behind the pergola from the Harry C. Hicks Studio in Los Angeles, requesting "tile that will show good strong coloring at a distance."[7] For the metalwork Ayres turned to Harold Russ Glick, a Southern California craftsman known for his ironwork and a member of the San Gabriel Artists Guild.[8]

Inside, the plastered walls of the principal spaces are painted white, strongly contrasting with the deep red floor tiles of various patterns, characteristic of Mediterranean houses. A distinctly different approach can be seen in the den, which features an abstractly patterned tile fireplace surround and is now decorated in a Moroccan style, with deep orange walls and kilim upholstery.

The rear garden is dominated by a rectangular pool. Several wall fountains add color and interest to the outdoor spaces: one off the side patio, another at the eastern edge of the pool, and a third attached to the wall that defines the outer edge of the driveway. Large mature trees, including oak, palm, ocotillo, and agave, are planted along the edges of the property.

Ayres and Ayres created a gracious residence for the Mannen family. It is of interest not only for its reflection of the firm's knowledge of Spanish architectural traditions but also for the ways Ayres and Ayres responded to San Antonio's semitropical climate by astutely siting the house and incorporating passive cooling methods.

Below: Den. Opposite: View from living room to reception hall

Above: Living room. Opposite: Street view

1. Everett, 115.

2. Ibid.

3. Pfeiffer and Pemberton-Haugh.

4. Mannen was named a "Hundred Pointer" sixteen of the nineteen years he worked for the company, meaning that he met the annual quota set by the home office. He began his stint in San Antonio in 1920, after having worked in several other offices of the company. E-mail messages to author from Jeff Opt, National Cash Register archivist for Dayton History, July 10 and 13, 2007.

5. "Old Spanish Ideas," *The American Architect* 135 (January 20, 1929), 132–38.

6. Coote, 91.

7. Atlee Ayres to Harry C. Hicks, February 2, 1927, Ayres Collection, Alexander Architectural Archive, University of Texas at Austin.

8. Barbara Miller, "Grandfather's Handicraft Lives Again," *Los Angeles Times*, July 28, 1935, E22.

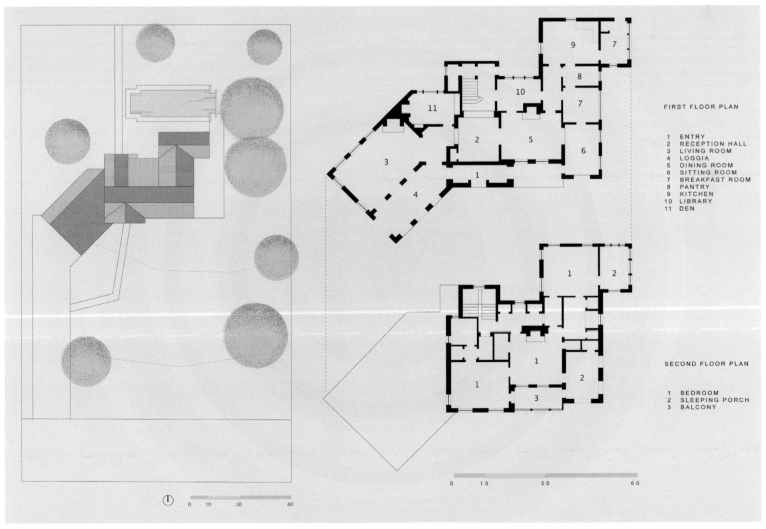

FIRST FLOOR PLAN

1 ENTRY
2 RECEPTION HALL
3 LIVING ROOM
4 LOGGIA
5 DINING ROOM
6 SITTING ROOM
7 BREAKFAST ROOM
8 PANTRY
9 KITCHEN
10 LIBRARY
11 DEN

SECOND FLOOR PLAN

1 BEDROOM
2 SLEEPING PORCH
3 BALCONY

0   10   30   60

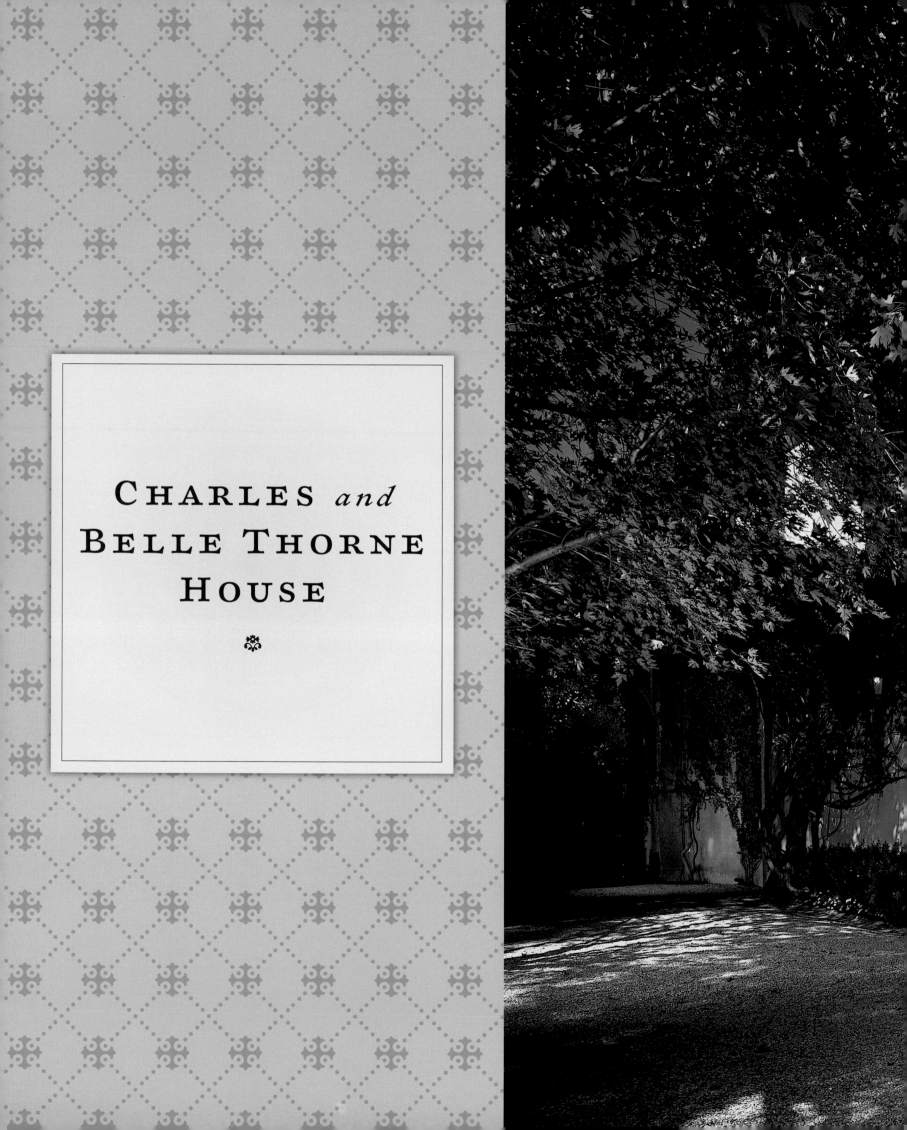

# CHARLES *and* BELLE THORNE HOUSE

Above: Rear view. Opposite: Entrance

NEAR THE TOP OF A PRIVATE ROAD PLANTED WITH ITALIAN STONE PINES
and lined with handsome stone retaining walls, the Charles and Belle Thorne house enjoys sweeping eastern views of the Arroyo Seco (a dry riverbed lined with native trees) and Pasadena, California.[1] The Thornes, who had decided to retire to the area (Charles Thorne had been president of Montgomery Ward), bought the property from fellow Chicagoan William S. Mason. They commissioned architect Wallace Neff about 1928, by which time Neff had established a reputation as one of Southern California's leading designers of suburban and country houses.

Like George Washington Smith (for whom he had briefly worked), Neff's studio-art training, refined aesthetic sense, and experience living abroad all contributed to an almost visceral understanding of the European and Mexican architecture that informed his work. Architectural historian Alson Clark described Neff's fifty-year practice as "a love of the rough and tumble rather than of the intellectual heights of the profession."[2]

Neff had a starry roster of Hollywood clients, including Mary Pickford and Douglas Fairbanks, Frederick March, and Darryl Zanuck. He also designed houses for industrialists such as King Gillette, of razor blade fame, and Edward L. Doheny, an oil tycoon. Though he often incorporated dramatic features such as curved exterior staircases and large sculptural openings, Neff's houses above all had a relaxed quality that became synonymous with a Californian life-style. For the Thornes he conceived a home that updated characteristic features of a Mexican hacienda to contemporary needs.

Above: View of courtyard. Opposite: Courtyard arcade

The Thorne house appears to have grown from its site. From its shady, gravel driveway all that can be seen is a long, simple wall with vegetation covering the scalloped parapet. A tall archway links the house to a two-story structure that contains the garage and an apartment. The front door to the house is a wrought-iron gate that opens to an arcaded loggia surrounding the central courtyard. The tile-roofed arcade may have been inspired by the historic Mission San Juan Capistrano in Orange County; a small tile scene of the mission is incorporated in one of the stucco walls enclosing the courtyard. The courtyard is carpeted with a rich green lawn and lushly framed by bougainvilleas, whose blossoms cover the loggia's columns and arches.

There are two primary routes of circulation: directly across the grassy courtyard to a second, glazed entry leading to the entrance hall and public rooms, or a less direct route along the tile-covered loggia, which leads to the bedroom suite to the south or the kitchen and service areas to the north, eventually arriving at the entrance hall and public rooms on the east side. Exterior circulation between rooms—characteristic of the Mexican adobe—is possible throughout the house. An outdoor dining room, complete with built-in barbeque, refrigerator, and dish cabinets, underscores the emphasis on outdoor living.

Restraint and simplicity characterize the interior. The virtually double-height living room has a large fireplace, tall enough to walk into.

On the opposite wall a pair of arched windows with glazed pocket doors frames a panorama of Pasadena. In most of the public rooms white plaster walls contrast with dark-stained wood-beam or wooden coffered ceilings. The house retains much of the integrity of its original design. Especially notable are the kitchen and pantry, which, with the exception of the wallpaper and a few updated appliances, retain their 1920s appearance.

A partial second floor provides more bedrooms, a loggia overlooking the courtyard, and a second balcony facing the spectacular eastern view. A small service yard is located off the kitchen, but otherwise there is limited space around the perimeter, as a portion of the land to the south was subdivided. However, a more extensive landscape is scarcely missed because of the open vistas.

---

1. The property is in the Alta San Rafael section of Pasadena, in a subdivision laid out by Olmsted Brothers in 1926.

2. Alson Clark, "Wallace Neff and the Culture of Los Angeles," in *Wallace Neff 1895–1982: The Romance of Regional Architecture*, 19.

Opposite: Living room. Above: Kitchen

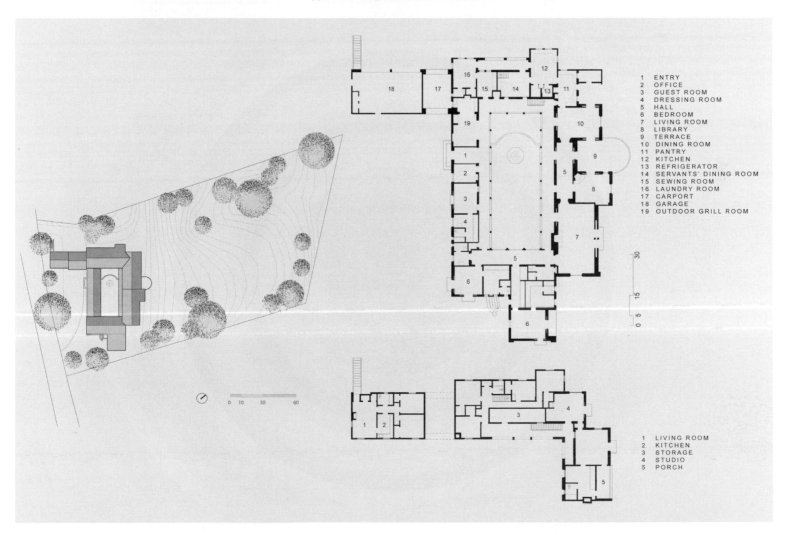

1  ENTRY
2  OFFICE
3  GUEST ROOM
4  DRESSING ROOM
5  HALL
6  BEDROOM
7  LIVING ROOM
8  LIBRARY
9  TERRACE
10 DINING ROOM
11 PANTRY
12 KITCHEN
13 REFRIGERATOR
14 SERVANTS' DINING ROOM
15 SEWING ROOM
16 LAUNDRY ROOM
17 CARPORT
18 GARAGE
19 OUTDOOR GRILL ROOM

1  LIVING ROOM
2  KITCHEN
3  STORAGE
4  STUDIO
5  PORCH

# Clark B. *and* Helen Staats Millikan House

Above: View from entry hall to living room. Opposite: Patio. Overleaf: Patio

THIS HOUSE, COMPLETED IN 1931, WAS WALLACE NEFF'S LAST MAJOR

commission before the Great Depression curtailed construction in the Pasadena area. Neff's clients were a socially and professionally prominent young couple with two sons. Clark Millikan was chairman of the department of aeronautical engineering at the California Institute for Technology and would be pivotal to Caltech's contribution to the growth of aeronautics in Southern California.[1] His wife, Helen, was highly creative, active in local theater in her youth, and interested in politics. She collaborated closely with Neff on the house design, and both took great pride in the final result; indeed, Neff considered it one of his most successful houses.

It was built on land Helen Millikan had inherited from her father, William R. Staats, who had made his fortune in real estate, oil, and utilities.[2] The property originally encompassed thirteen acres of canyon land in northwest Pasadena. Neff graded a scrub-covered site perched over a steep drop, capturing magnificent views of the city. The San Gabriel Mountains to the north serve as the house's backdrop.

Borrowing from the Mediterranean courtyard tradition, Neff designed a house that embraced the outdoors yet had a warm, protective quality. That duality is apparent from the first step onto the property, at the motor court: The house is enclosed on two sides by solid white stucco walls that are animated by the shadows cast by olive trees. A pair of large blue doors opens onto a central, paved courtyard with a covered walkway around all four sides; originally a single pepper tree provided a note of asymmetry here. A modestly sized door at the courtyard's northeast corner leads to the main entrance hall.

An arched opening in the hallway gives on to the dramatic two-story living room, spanned by a pair of massive trusses. On the same grand scale, a pair of Spanish doors—almost fifteen feet tall—leads to a curved terrace. Between these doors stands a double fireplace, which provides a focal point for the living room and makes an outdoor room of the terrace. Above the interior fireplace Helen Millikan had placed a large Mexican plate she purchased on Olvera Street near the historic Plaza of Los Angeles, the oldest part of the city; it now hangs over the main entrance.

The terrace runs most of the length of the house. A covered section with arched openings has been carefully enclosed by large steel-framed glass doors. An English garden, the lawn edged by a variety of flowering plants, now unfolds below the terrace, but the Millikans had kept the native scrub as ground cover, except for a small, formal garden at the south end. The Millikans also cleared trails through the canyons, where the father, sons, and their dogs went walking on Sundays.

Clark Millikan's study occupied the northeast corner of the house; heavy dark beams and a curved corner fireplace make it a warm, intimate space. At the opposite end of the house, the dining and breakfast rooms are simply detailed spaces with multiple views to the outdoors. They demonstrate Neff's approach, as the Millikans' son Michael described it: "He imposed nothing upon you but designed it so that the mood was created by whatever the people therein were doing."[3] Bedrooms and service quarters are well considered, but the life of the house was clearly centered on the communal space.

Above: Living room. Below: Study. Opposite: Loggia (now enclosed)

The atmosphere of that space would vary, depending on the family activity, Michael Millikan recollected. "It could be full of warmth and even coziness. It could be grand, formal, and almost austere. It could be intense, as when there were stimulating and heated discussions about world affairs, science, art, or esoteric subject[s]. It could be extremely happy, as it was with the festive parties my parents would give."[4] Such versatility was typical of Neff's work. For the Millikans, as for many other clients, he created an eminently livable, comfortable house.

1. See Ernest E. Sechler, "Clark Blanchard Millikan," in *Memorial Tributes: National Academy of Engineering*, vol. 1 (Washington, D.C.: The Academy, 1979), 213. Millikan was a son of Robert Millikan, the physicist and Nobel laureate who was chairman of Caltech's executive council in 1921–46.

2. Carol Green Wilson, *California Yankee: William R. Staats Business Pioneer* (Claremont, Calif.: Saunders Press, 1946).

3. Michael Millikan, "Reflections on 1500 Normandy Drive," ms. in author's collection, September 2001.

4. Ibid.

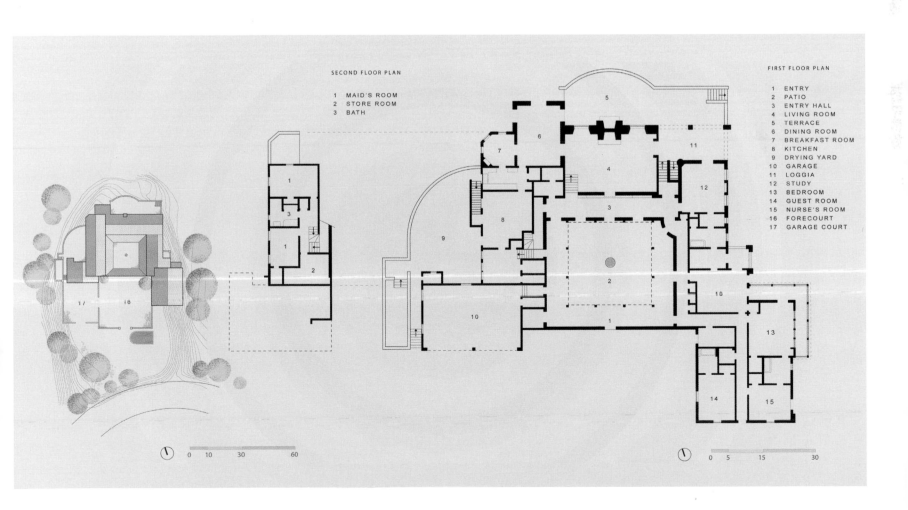

SECOND FLOOR PLAN

1 MAID'S ROOM
2 STORE ROOM
3 BATH

FIRST FLOOR PLAN

1 ENTRY
2 PATIO
3 ENTRY HALL
4 LIVING ROOM
5 TERRACE
6 DINING ROOM
7 BREAKFAST ROOM
8 KITCHEN
9 DRYING YARD
10 GARAGE
11 LOGGIA
12 STUDY
13 BEDROOM
14 GUEST ROOM
15 NURSE'S ROOM
16 FORECOURT
17 GARAGE COURT

0 10 30 60

0 5 15 30

# KEMPER
# CAMPBELL
# RANCH

Above: Patio. Opposite: Entry, with view to living room. Overleaf: Living room

THIS CLASSIC ADOBE HOUSE IN VICTORVILLE, CALIFORNIA, frames an eastern vista of ranchland that extends to the Mojave River, an extraordinary desert landscape studded with Joshua and cottonwood trees, but with marshlands close to the river that make it ideal for grazing cattle. The ranch is not only tailored to its location, climate, and topography like the best-designed Mediterranean houses; it literally could not exist anywhere else, as its adobe walls grew from the soil on site. Adobe's ability to retain heat (minimizing swings in the interior temperature) makes it perfect for the ranch's desert setting, where temperatures reach 110 degrees in the summer and drop by approximately 30 degrees at night.

The architect was John Byers, who was well established in Santa Monica by 1928–29, when Kemper and Litta Belle Campbell commissioned him to design a country house on the Verde Ranch (established in 1858), a cattle ranch they had purchased several years earlier. A native of Michigan, Byers trained as an electrical engineer but taught Romance languages in Uruguay and Northern California before moving to Santa Monica. There he established a company that produced adobe bricks and handmade tiles. He soon began designing adobe residences and became a licensed architect in 1926.[1] Though he worked in a range of styles (he produced an English-Norman farmhouse for Shirley Temple in 1935–36), Byers was expert in adobe construction, of which he said,

*While every permanent material of which houses are built may have written its own romance down through the ages, it is doubtful if any can lay claim to a more interesting past than this very simple, sun-baked mud brick. . . . Buildings of adobe are replete with a delicate and elusive charm and there is an easy plasticity about the material that makes it particularly suitable to the Spanish, or California, type of architecture.[2]*

The ranch house encapsulated Byers's view of historic adobes' aesthetic appeal: "The long low simple lines, the play of light and shadow on the walls, the soft colorful texture of the roofs, the sincerity of design and composition of primitive adobe structure are almost impossible to improve upon architecturally, or otherwise."[3] The linear building is made up of distinctive components, as it developed over time in response to the Campbells' need for additional space. The two-story, virtually solid section at the south end is balanced by a single-story portion with a porch that anchors the house to its site. Later, an old house was moved to the site and attached to the original dwelling, defining the western edge of the central patio.[4] Byers visually linked this part with the existing structure by sheathing its exterior with adobe bricks and running a second-story balcony across the facade, aligning it with the original stair landing. (With later additions, there were eleven bedrooms in the main residence; the accompanying plan, showing six bedrooms, represents principally the early construction.)

The ranch buildings were constructed with traditional methods and materials. The adobe bricks, fourteen inches by twenty inches, were made on site by Mexican workers of water-soaked local soil, straw, manure, and dried grass. The mixture was poured into molds (*adoberas*), kneaded by hand, and left to dry in the sun. Then bricks were carefully turned over the next two weeks to dry them thoroughly before construction. They were laid over a poured concrete foundation with mud mortar.

In 1929 writer Marc N. Goodnow contended that adobe construction held unique aesthetic value.

*In the hands of a trained craftsman, this type of building material lends itself to picturesque effects of traditional and historic beauty. Because of the character of the bricks themselves, it is, of course, less prim and precise; but there is an easy plasticity about it that makes it particularly suitable to the Spanish type of architecture. It seems to call for dignity rather than temperamental jazz in its expression, but for all that it is a spontaneous medium, sometimes evoking a surprising quality of humanness.[5]*

Bedroom

Byers left the adobe bricks exposed at the Kemper Campbell Ranch, maintaining that the only protection they needed in extremely dry climates was a wide overhanging eave and/or a plaster dado about three feet tall at the base of the exterior.[6] (He often painted or white-washed his adobes in Los Angeles.) Two-foot exposed rafter ends constructed of old railroad ties form a protective roof extension supported by a row of six beams. The beams came from oil derricks, but Litta Campbell's father, David Hibben, worked them with a draw knife for a hand-hewn appearance.[7] Hibben is also credited with using rubbing posts from the pasture—smoothed by generations of cattle—for the railing of the balcony that overlooks the double-height living room.[8]

Construction began shortly before the stock market crash of October 1929. Over time the Campbells added other buildings to the prop-erty, creating an ensemble that reflected the Spanish and, more specifi-cally, the Mexican adobe ranch tradition. An office and playhouse were added to the north end of the patio and the south end of the house, respectively, and eventually were joined by an apartment, a separate residence for the Campbells' daughter and son-in-law, a swimming pool, tennis courts, and a pergola roofed with tule mats.

The Kemper Campbell Ranch was a twentieth-century South-western counterpart to the sixteenth-century Italian villa, a rustic retreat for sophisticated urbanites. The Campbells were high-powered attorneys for whom it represented escape.[9] Initially the family spent long summer vacations at the ranch; about 1932 the children moved there, and the parents joined them on weekends.[10] (In 1943 the eldest son, Kemper Campbell Jr., was killed while completing military train-ing; the ranch was named in his memory.)

The Campbells weathered the economic downtown of the 1930s, but friends and associates in Los Angeles asked if they could visit the ranch as paying guests, in lieu of more expensive vacations. In 1933 the Campbells began charging guests five dollars a day or twenty-five dollars a week, including meals, swimming, tennis, and horseback riding. They operated the guest ranch until 1975, hosting such celebrities as Greer Garson, Groucho Marx, John Wayne, and Greta Garbo; also at the ranch Herman Mankiewicz completed the screenplay of *Citizen Kane* and J. B. Priestly wrote part of *Midnight on the Desert.*

1. David Gebhard, Lauren Weiss Bricker, and David Bricker, *A Catalogue of the Architectural Drawing Collection* (University of California Santa Barbara: University Art Museum, 1983), 74.

2. "Romance Seen in Adobe Brick," *Los Angeles Times*, May 17, 1931, D4.

3. Ibid.

4. Interview with Joseph Campbell and Jean De Blasis by Leo Lyman, Carolyn Clark, and Carolyn Haughton, March 23, 1990, transcribed by Leslie Huiner (www.empirenet.com/rdthompson/interviewcampbelldeblasis.html, June 23, 2007). Joseph Campbell recounts how a team of horses dragged the house to the site.

5. Goodnow, 38.

6. John Byers, "At Home on the Desert," *California Arts and Architecture* 22:4 (October 1937), 17.

7. Campbell and De Blasis interview.

8. Martha L. Brindley, "The Mojave Desert Inspired this Architecture," *Arts and Decoration* 51:1 (October 1939), 17.

9. Kemper was active in reforming the Los Angeles County court system, helped establish the State Bar of California, and was an officer of the Los Angeles County and American Bar associations. Litta Belle began practicing law with her future husband soon after graduating from USC Law School (John G. Tomlinson, "Shoulder to Shoulder: Litta Belle Hibben Campbell and Women of the USC Law School during the Early Years," *USC Law*, Spring 1997, 7). She temporarily left the practice for an appointment as deputy district attorney—the first woman in the nation to hold such a position. After purchasing the ranch, Kemper also bred cattle and Arabian horses ("Kemper Campbell, Long Civic Leader, Dies at 75," *Los Angeles Times*, January 9, 1957, C10).

10. Interview with Mrs. Kemper Campbell by Ruth Smith, transcribed by Angela Hamilton, December 8, 1970, Mohahave Historical Society Oral Histories (www.empirenet.com/rdthompson/interviewcampbelllitta.html, June 23, 2007).

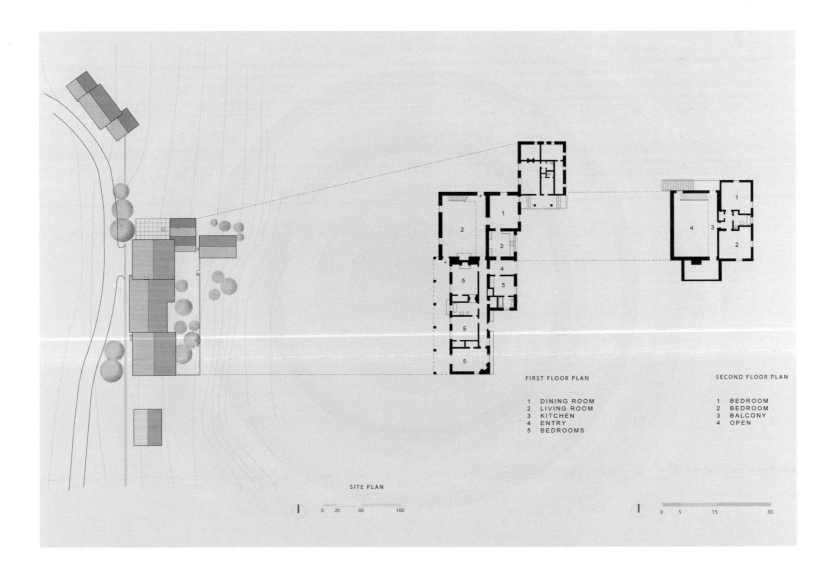

SITE PLAN

0 20 60 100

FIRST FLOOR PLAN

1 DINING ROOM
2 LIVING ROOM
3 KITCHEN
4 ENTRY
5 BEDROOMS

SECOND FLOOR PLAN

1 BEDROOM
2 BEDROOM
3 BALCONY
4 OPEN

0 5 15 30

# EVA KATHARINE FUDGER HOUSE

❖

Above: Street view. Opposite: View of entrance and motor court

THE MONTEREY HOUSE IS A TWO-STORY REGIONAL HOUSE TYPE THAT
emerged in California in the 1920s, updating the adobe tradition, often with conventional wood-frame construction. Architect Roland E. Coate played a seminal role in its development, and the house he designed for Eva Katharine Fudger in 1926 is one of the most important essays in what he called the "Early California House."[1] A relatively early example of the type, the house has a primitive, handmade quality that evokes nineteenth-century adobes. The Monterey house would continue to evolve in the 1930s, with lighter wood treatments—milled lumber for balconies, shake roof, wooden interior floors—that were characteristic of Northern California and presented less a Spanish image than an Anglo one.

A transplanted Midwesterner by way of New York, Coate arrived in Los Angeles in 1919. After partnering with Reginald Johnson and Gordon B. Kaufmann—largely producing houses and churches—Coate opened his own office in 1925, with a residential focus. Many of his 1920s projects were in Pasadena and the Los Angeles area. In the 1930s and early 1940s, as the region's financial strength shifted to the movie industry, Coate's practice gravitated toward the areas where Hollywood types were settling, including Beverly Hills, Holmby Hills, and Brentwood.

The Fudger house is in Hancock Park, an upper-middle-class subdivision in the Wilshire district, several miles west of downtown Los Angeles. It was developed on land owned by the petroleum magnate G. Allan Hancock[2] and bordering the Wilshire Country Club's golf course,[3] making it an especially valuable piece of real estate. Fudger, whose father was a prominent businessman, was a widow who shared the house with her two daughters and was active in civic and philanthropic affairs. After

she moved to another house Coate designed for her, it is believed that Howard Hughes made the house his own.[4]

Originally the H-shaped house was visible from the street—presenting the essential horizontality and distinctive cantilevered balcony that are hallmarks of the Monterey style—but it is now obscured by a grove of olive trees in the front yard and a tall Eugenia hedge. A stone-paved driveway leads under an overpass linking the house and garage/chauffeur's quarters (now an office and apartment), then to a motor court at the secluded entrance facade. The radiating surface pattern of concrete with stone infill makes the motor court a formal space befitting the main entrance. In contrast with the horizontality of the street facade, the entrance facade is an informal vertical composition of cubic volumes sheltering the front door.

The interiors are extremely simple, characteristic of the early Monterey style, which makes it a versatile backdrop for a wide range of decorative treatments and furnishings, though there are vernacular details: The entrance hall floor is covered with terra-cotta tiles, while the staircase risers are adorned with decorative blue and white glazed tiles. White plastered walls contrast with heavy, hand-hewn beams in the living room. The dining room features a stone fireplace and deep molding at the ceiling. On the second floor, large plate-glass windows, added in the 1970s, capture the master bedroom's views of the golf course—a prime selling point.

Coate typically preferred to involve the landscape architect (in this case, Florence Yoch) at the very beginning of a project—and the fluid integration of the Fudger house and its garden, both designed in 1926 and completed the following year, suggests the advantages

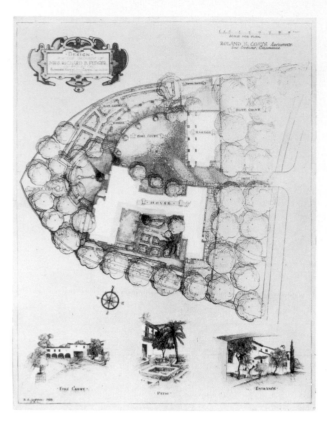

Archival site plan. c. 1926. Huntington Library, San Marino, California

of doing so. The plan reflects their shared fascination with the Mediterranean courtyard tradition. But as Yoch noted, most city dwellers in Southern California found themselves too busy to spend much time living outdoors, despite the appeal of doing so. Therefore, she wrote, the architect must "provide for this contingency by designing a house which brings the outdoors in as close as possible relation to every day living" by incorporating patios, terraces, pergolas, loggias, and balconies, elements that link the "architect's work and that of the landscape man."[5]

Many of these devices were used at the Fudger house. Upon entering the visitor sees the deep loggia—which links the living room and the central patio—with its reflected outdoor light. The dining room opens directly to the garden; the kitchen, enclosing the eastern edge of the patio, has been altered to have a more open relationship to the garden. Coate also took every opportunity to open the second story to the outdoors, with a sleeping porch above the loggia, a cantilevered balcony hall projecting above the dining room, and an exterior staircase leading to the servant's quarters.

Opposite: Loggia. Above: Dining room. Below: Living room

Above: Bathroom with view to bedroom. Below: Bedroom. Opposite: Entrance hall

Yoch conceived the patio as an outdoor room, with a fountain, planting beds, and several trees; her spare use of water and selection of plants reveal a familiarity with the Moorish gardens of Spain. Today, dense vegetation dominates, with the simple walls of cement stucco receding behind it. Steps wrap around the exterior and finally descend into an arch-shaped pergola at the rear of the property. An olive grove and rose garden were planted in the backyard. A pool and surrounding terrace were added in the 1970s.

Numerous publications featured the Fudger house soon after its completion. It received an Honor Award from the Southern California Chapter of the American Institute of Architects in 1930 for "skill and interest of design in a peculiarly shaped lot."[6]

1. Roland E. Coate, "The Early California House: Blending Colonial and California Forms," *California Arts and Architecture* 35 (March 1929), 20–30.

2. Moye W. Stephens, "A Concrete Example," *Los Angeles Times*, August 27, 1922, V10. Hancock also owned the land encompassing the world-famous La Brea Tar Pits, which he donated to Los Angeles County to create a public park. "Deed to Hancock Park is Given to County," *Los Angeles Times*, December 12, 1916, Section 2, 1–2.

3. Hancock had donated 115 acres for the club's development. "Splendid New Close in Country Club is Planned for Wilshire Region," *Los Angeles Times*, July 27, 1919, V11.

4. Fudger sold her property to Archie A. MacDonald, manager of the Hughes Tool Company, presumably on behalf of Howard Hughes, the company's owner, who is believed to have occupied the house during the late 1940s. Tim Gregory, unpublished ms., 2006, in author's collection.

5. Florence Yoch, "Fitting the Land for Human Use," *California Arts and Architecture*, July 1930, 21.

6. Quoted in James J. Yoch, *Landscaping the American Dream: The Gardens and Film Sets of Florence Yoch: 1890–1972* (New York: Harry N. Abrams, Inc., 1989), 49.

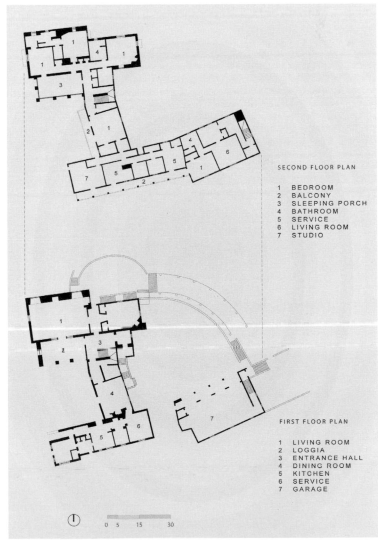

SECOND FLOOR PLAN

1 BEDROOM
2 BALCONY
3 SLEEPING PORCH
4 BATHROOM
5 SERVICE
6 LIVING ROOM
7 STUDIO

FIRST FLOOR PLAN

1 LIVING ROOM
2 LOGGIA
3 ENTRANCE HALL
4 DINING ROOM
5 KITCHEN
6 SERVICE
7 GARAGE

0  5   15    30

# Nicholas *and* Maria del Pilar Bates House

Above: Interior courtyard view. Opposite: Garden view

## COLONIAL REVIVAL AND TUDOR STYLES DOMINATE THE LEAFY STREETS

of Riverdale, New York, a residential neighborhood of the Bronx at the northern reaches of New York City. The four-season climate, with its extreme summers and winters, certainly does not evoke the Mediterranean, nor is it conducive to year-round indoor-outdoor living. Nevertheless, Riverdale has its share of Mediterranean houses, adapted to and blending with the location. One is the house Dwight James Baum designed for Nicholas Bates, president of the Bronx Motors Distributing Company, his wife, Maria, and their six children. The couple reportedly had lived for a number of years in Mexico City, which may have influenced their choice of what was described as a "Mexican house."[1]

Baum, a leading residential architect of the 1920s and 1930s, built his own home and designed more than a hundred others in Riverdale. He was known for his ability to design in a range of styles and for different incomes: His first "magazine house" was a middle-class Spanish residence published in *Ladies Home Journal* in 1923, but in 1927 he designed a Venetian palace for John and Mable Ringling in Sarasota, Florida, now the John and Mable Ringling Museum of Art. He had an early, pronounced interest in the Mediterranean house, writing perceptively in 1918 about architecture in Southern California, where he found "a new style based on partly Spanish and partly Italian precedent."[2] While acknowledging that the Mediterranean style looked "so much at home" in Florida and California,[3] Baum was open to siting such a house in the Northeast's entirely different context, even next door to a Colonial. The challenge would be to "satisfy the individual preferences of the owner, and at the same time harmonize well with the adjoining dwellings."[4] An article in *Country Life* explained his sensitive approach.

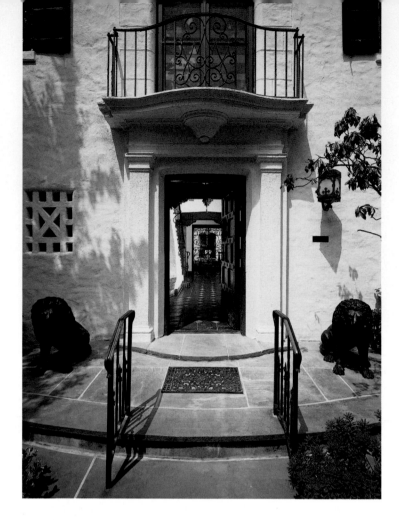

Above: Entrance. Above right: Living room fireplace. Opposite: Entrance hall

*Mr. Baum says that his practice is to fit the style to the person and to the landscape. He looks over the site and environment and determines what style house it is possible to build there, and then he goes to visit his client at home and tries to judge what style of architecture is particularly suited to him. Finally, when he begins to design he strives to make this house, whatever type it may be, as good or better than houses designed by architects who specialize in this particular type.[5]*

Part of the Bates house's success can be attributed to its site plan and landscape treatment. The house sits on a pie-shaped corner parcel. In response, Baum created a wide U-shaped plan that wraps around three sides of a courtyard patio and echoes the three sides of the lot. Tall, densely planted mature trees frame the entrance and partially screen the house. The entrance facade, to the south, is virtually parallel with the street, and the secondary, garage exposure faces the curve in the road to the east. The transition between the formally symmetrical entrance facade and the informal side elevation is made through a series of setbacks, a sculptural exposed chimney, and roof planes covered with terra-cotta tile.

Baum's attention to detail imbues the design with a convincingly Mediterranean character. The entrance is given prominence by a sculpted plaster surround and a projecting second-story balcony with a wrought-iron railing Baum designed.[6] He also designed the wrought-iron window grilles on the first-floor, the railings of the entrance hall balcony, and the gate separating the hall from the loggia. Most of the floors are covered with old tiles from Spanish monasteries. In the courtyard, a tile-covered wall fountain (since removed) was decorated with tiles that Baum designed and had made in Spain. The courtyard originally was illuminated with a blue floodlight, adding to the "romance of moonlight."[7]

In the rooms on the first floor, the extreme simplicity of the plaster walls contrasts with the lavish use of tile on floors, walls, the living room fireplace overmantel, and built-in benches in the hall and loggia. The entrance hall links to the loggia, which Baum, adapting Mediterranean precedent, treated as a transitional space between the living room and the courtyard. Here, however, the loggia has a more substantial, weathertight separation from the outdoors than seen in houses in California and Florida: Brick piers frame a series of French doors with wooden grilles covering semicircular transoms. The courtyard is

Above left: Loggia. Above right: Archival view of fountain patio. 1929. Gottscho Photography.
Avery Architectural & Fine Arts Library, Columbia University, New York. Below: Living room, opening to loggia

treated as an outdoor room, but one with a decidedly East Coast feel, with stucco and whitewashed brick walls, a bay window with hand-hewn half-timber detailing, and lush vines growing on the upper walls. The dining room retains the simplicity of its original design, the fireplace and built-in cabinetry being the principal decorative features.

Upstairs, one of the two principal bedrooms has been converted to a stately office, rich in wall coverings and furnishings. The remaining bedrooms have a spare, airy quality. A hallway lined by windows onto the courtyard leads to three additional bedrooms, and a rear hallway at the north end provides access to what may have been a servant's bedroom.

With the Bates house, Baum demonstrated the adaptability of the Mediterranean style to a Northeastern context, creating a house that is appropriate to the site, the climate, and its residents' needs. Is it, strictly speaking, Mediterranean? A 1927 monograph on Baum's works, which labels houses like Bates the "Italian type," offers an interesting view: that such houses represented an *American* type, whose plan, construction, materials, and equipment are "as different from an Italian villa as . . . from an Eskimo's igloo," though it is logical "to call [such] a house of the Italian type, since the Italian villa was its point of departure."[8]

1. "A House in the Spanish Manner," *Country Life* 58:6 (October 1930), 57.

2. Dwight James Baum, "An Eastern Architect's Impressions of Recent Work in Southern California," *Architecture* 38:1 (July 1918), 177.

3. Dwight James Baum, "When You Choose the Style of Your House Here are the Things to Consider," *Good Housekeeping* 90:6 (June 1930), 57.

4. Ibid., 183.

5. Joseph Cummings Chase, "Discussed by Dwight James Baum," *Country Life* 52 (October 1927), 53.

6. Baum's wrought-iron work is the subject "Drafting for Metal Work, Part V: Working Drawings for Wrought Iron Balconies, Grilles and Railings from the Office of Dwight James Baum, Architect," *The Metal Arts* 2:2 (April 1929), 165–72, 179.

7. "A House in the Spanish Manner," 58.

8. Price, n. p.

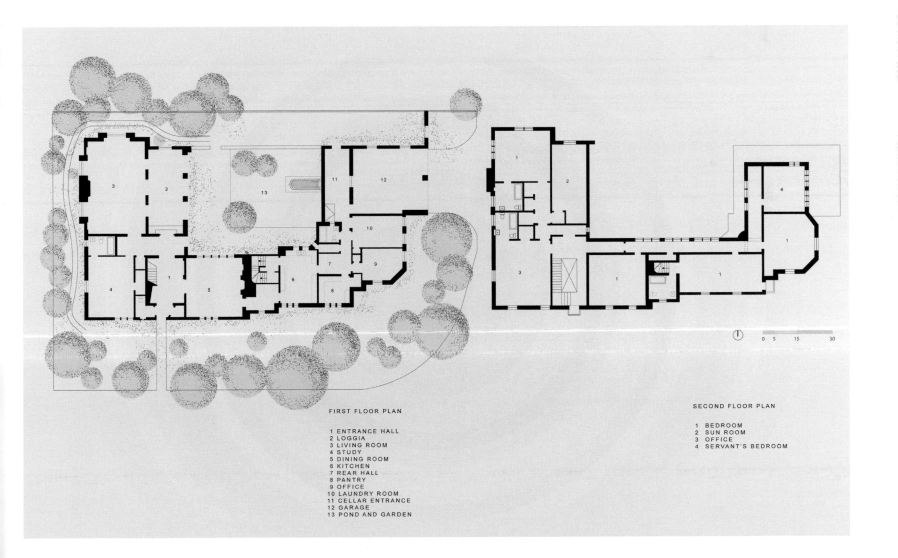

FIRST FLOOR PLAN

1 ENTRANCE HALL
2 LOGGIA
3 LIVING ROOM
4 STUDY
5 DINING ROOM
6 KITCHEN
7 REAR HALL
8 PANTRY
9 OFFICE
10 LAUNDRY ROOM
11 CELLAR ENTRANCE
12 GARAGE
13 POND AND GARDEN

SECOND FLOOR PLAN

1 BEDROOM
2 SUN ROOM
3 OFFICE
4 SERVANT'S BEDROOM

# VILLA FLORA

*Edward and Flora*

*Shearson House*

Above: Oceanside facade. Opposite: Cloister. Overleaf: Living room

PALM BEACH, FLORIDA, WAS BUILT FOR PLEASURE. BY THE MID-1910S
it was a "dream of blazing flower-gardens and allées of palms," where "not to be rich was a state unworthy and discreditable and thus not to be mentioned before nice people. The elite led secluded lives in private estates."[1]

The architect widely credited with creating the quintessential house for this luxury-loving, seasonal resort is Addison Mizner. When Mizner arrived, in 1918, he found its visitors reluctant to build houses they would use for only a few weeks each year; he "saw it was necessary to change the life at Palm Beach and . . . worked toward that end."[2] With the financial backing of Paris Singer, heir to the sewing machine fortune, Mizner began to imprint his architectural vision on the city, beginning with the swanky and exclusive Everglades Club (1918). His houses became popular seemingly overnight. Sensing a burgeoning market, other architects soon established practices catering to Palm Beach's seasonal residents.

Spain was Mizner's design inspiration, less because of Florida's Spanish colonial history (the nearest architectural remnants of Spanish settlement were three hundred miles away, in Saint Augustine) than because

> Northern [that is, Colonial Revival] architecture didn't register there. . . . It couldn't hold its own in that strong color and light, and with the cocoanut trees hanging over the front door. It certainly looked absurd. . . . I based my design largely on the old architecture of Spain—with important modifications to meet Florida conditions and modern ways of living. I studied architecture of Spain itself, and drew somewhat on my knowledge of Spanish tropical America.[3]

Though Mizner was entranced by historic architecture, he drew upon it in romantic and unorthodox ways, mixing and matching to elaborate effect.

> *Most modern architects have spent their lives carrying out a period to the last letter and producing a characterless copybook effect. My ambition has been to take the reverse stand—to make a building look traditional and as though it had fought its way from a small unimportant structure to a great rambling house that took centuries of different needs and up and downs of wealth to accomplish. I sometimes start a house with a Romanesque corner, pretend that it has fallen into disrepair and been added to in the Gothic spirit, when suddenly the great wealth of the New World has poured in and the owner had added a very rich Renaissance addition.*[4]

Mizner's Palm Beach style is beautifully exemplified in Villa Flora (1923), one of his most important houses there. It was built for Edward Shearson and his wife, Flora, for whom it was named. Shearson, a successful stockbroker, had founded the firm of Shearson, Hammill & Company in 1902.[5] The twelve-thousand-square-foot house sits at the north end of Palm Beach, with beach frontage on the Atlantic Ocean. Its permit value was eighty thousand dollars (though Mizner's budgets usually exceeded the initial estimate)—relatively modest compared with some of Mizner's other projects. Shearson reportedly convinced Mizner to adjust his costs for "frugal financiers who 'wanted houses for only three or four weeks a year.'"[6]

Villa Flora's U-shaped floor plan was loosely derived from the Spanish patio house, but its exterior decorative features are associated with the Venetian Gothic. In contrast to the fairly solid walls of the traditional Spanish house, Mizner provided multiple and varied window openings "to let the sunshine and air into the house, and, in other ways, make people feel that they were living out-of-doors."[7] The overall horizontal massing is broken up by subtle variations of roof heights and projecting chimney stacks; Mizner believed Florida's flat landscape demanded the visual interest of a picturesque roof profile.

The entrance, at the north end, leads to a long "cloister"—a hallway lined on one side by arched openings to the living room and on the other by a bank of windows and double French doors to a terrace. The Venetian ogee arches repeat on the arcade's exterior windows and in a

Above: Terrace and patio. Opposite top: Dining room. Opposite bottom: Bedroom

series of blind arches above the windows facing the terrace: From the terrace (now covered by a canopy), shallow steps descend to a stone-paved patio with a lush composition of palms and other tropical plants. A pool was added to the northwest corner of the property.

The interiors are characterized by rich materials that appear to be worn by time. In fact, most (if not all) of the materials and furniture were manufactured in West Palm Beach by Mizner's own companies. At the time Mizner designed Villa Flora and his other great houses, no local firm produced the materials he considered essential to the Mediterranean style—terra-cotta roof tiles, ceramic floor tiles, decorative iron-work, marble, glass, and carved wooden details—so he established his

own. Las Manos Potteries at first manufactured roof tiles[8] but quickly expanded into Mizner Industries, which made pottery, wrought-iron grilles, gates, lanterns, andirons, hardware, and, by 1923, reproductions of antique furniture. Mizner's discovery of pecky cypress, whose porous surface could be worked and painted to appear old, contributed to his interiors' antique character.[9] He used pecky cypress for Villa Flora's massive front door and the wooden beams in the living and dining rooms.

Mizner expressly designed Villa Flora for resort life, accommodating casual daytime activity as well as formal dinners and entertainment. Perhaps more important, he paid sharp attention to passive cooling methods. The house is oriented to take advantage of prevailing breezes

Above: Terrace. Below left: Pool. Below right: Staircase

from the ocean and from the south, and it is one room deep, encouraging natural ventilation. The living room, with views to the ocean, is brilliantly lit in the morning, but in the heat of the afternoon the sunshine is cooled as it passes through the shade of the cloister before reaching the adjacent living room. The first-story cloister is repeated on the second floor, providing afternoon shade for the bedrooms. Other methods of controlling the interior temperature were the tile floors and spare use of rugs and curtains, high ceilings that allow warm air to escape, and tinted and stained-glass windows that protect the house from the ocean's glare. Such practical considerations may be overshadowed by the flourish of the architectural imagery, but they demonstrate Mizner's understanding of the aptness of the Mediterranean style for Florida.

1. Harrison Rhodes, *In Vacation America* (New York: Harper, 1915), 116.

2. Boyd, 80.

3. Ibid., 39–40.

4. Quoted in Ida M. Tarbell, "Addison Mizner Appreciation of a Layman," *Florida Architecture of Addison Mizner* (New York: Dover Publications, Inc., 1992 reprint of 1928 edition), xxxix.

5. "Edward Shearson, A Stockbroker, 86," *New York Times*, November 1, 1950, 35.

6. Shirley Johnson, *Palm Beach Houses* (New York: Rizzoli, 1991), 134.

7. Boyd, 80.

8. Curl, 53–54.

9. Mizner also developed a process to reproduce wooden ceilings, doors, and panels in "Woodite"—a pulpy composite of wood shavings, plaster of Paris, and fibrous material. The mixture was poured into plaster cast molds and when dry could be stained, painted, nailed, or sawed like wood. See Curl, 56.

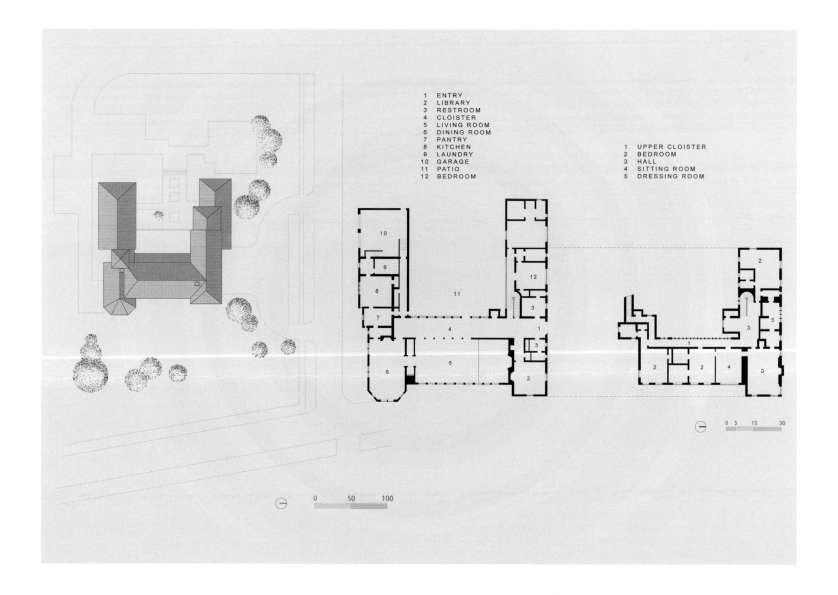

1  ENTRY
2  LIBRARY
3  RESTROOM
4  CLOISTER
5  LIVING ROOM
6  DINING ROOM
7  PANTRY
8  KITCHEN
9  LAUNDRY
10  GARAGE
11  PATIO
12  BEDROOM

1  UPPER CLOISTER
2  BEDROOM
3  HALL
4  SITTING ROOM
5  DRESSING ROOM

# CASA DELLA PORTA

*Mrs. and Mrs. William J. McAneeny House*

Above: Pool view. Opposite: Entry

BY THE MID-1920S MEMBERS OF THE SOCIAL AND FINANCIAL ELITE
of the Northeast and upper Midwest were clamoring for villas in Palm Beach where they could luxuriate during the winter
months. Perhaps the most talented of the young designers who arrived to meet the demand was Maurice Fatio, a Swiss-born
architect who practiced in New York before opening a Palm Beach office with William A. Treanor in 1924. Fatio considered
Casa della Porta, built for Mr. and Mrs. William J. McAneeny in 1928–29, "the greatest house I have ever done."[1]

The Mediterranean villa is named for its monumental stone entrance, whose broad lintel is inscribed *Casa della Porta
del Paradiso* (House of the Door of Paradise, an allusion to Lorenzo Ghiberti's famous doors to the Baptistery in Florence).
Fatio drew inspiration from the Italian Romanesque but at the same time prominently used a local material, coquina stone
quarried near the Florida Keys, deftly translating the foreign past into the Floridian present. Coquina stone (a porous limestone) sheathes the exterior and is used for many important interior features, including the courtyard's arches, columns with
carved capitals, and paving. The stone's surface is impressed with fossilized marine vegetation, underscoring the association
of the house and its tropical setting. Architecture critic Augusta Owen Patterson said of coquina stone, "As it is coral stone,
the moss gets into it; the seeds of the parasitic vegetation cling to the moss, with the result that a plant of the orchid variety
may be seen growing incredibly out of a wall."[2] Casa della Porta was the first Palm Beach house to make such extensive use of
coquina, though the stone had been widely used for commercial buildings in nearby Coral Gables during the 1920s.

Opposite: View from north loggia across courtyard. Above: East loggia

Casa della Porta is imposing from the first view, its massive masonry form and high-quality stone carving around the entrance inspiring awe. Fatio composed the house of large, simple, asymmetrical masses, breaking up its great size by recessing various sections. A three-story tower steps back from the facade at the southeast corner of the building; its simplicity of form and Romanesque details, such as the pairs of round-headed windows, recall a medieval campanile. The grand salon is set beyond the tower and lit by pointed arched windows. The dining room, slightly recessed to the west of the entry, also is pierced by pairs of large arched windows.

The house's external, protective solidity gives way to extremely open space inside. The largest living area is the courtyard, eighty-five

feet square, with arched loggias on its east and north sides and arched windows to the south, a continuous arcade that suggested a medieval cloister to writers who described the house at its completion. Fatio varied the treatment of the loggias: The eastern one is divided into five bays by composite piers with carved capitals and is covered with a groin-vaulted ceiling. Its flooring combines Cuban tile with coquina stone inset in a diamond pattern. On the north side, the loggia's five bays are divided by single columns with carved capitals. It has a complex wood-beamed ceiling in the Moorish tradition.

The principal public rooms are distributed around the courtyard. The entrance hall, with its fluid sweep of coquina stone steps and wrought-iron railing, is at the base of the tower. The grand salon occupies most of the

Above: Dining room. Below: Grand salon. Opposite left: Entrance hall. Opposite right: Gallery, opening to dining room and breakfast room. Overleaf: Pool room

eastern wing; despite its imposing dimensions (forty-five feet by twenty-six feet), it conveys a warm domesticity owing to its linen-fold wood paneling, Jacobean ceiling, and built-in bookcases (some of which once concealed a pipe organ and a Prohibition-era bar). The conversational seating arrangements (still used today as they were in the 1920s) and the baronial fireplace subdivide the room, making it feel more intimate.

Contemporary articles indicated the McAneenys sought to avoid the theatricality and ostentation of other large Palm Beach houses. While they were people of considerable means—he was president of Hudson Motor Car Company and later of Hupp Motor Car Corporation—they desired a comfortable house for themselves and their two children.[3] Working with New York interior designer Ruth Campbell Bigelow they selected an "Early English" decorative scheme, imbuing Fatio's grand interiors with great beauty without being "gorgeously exhibitional."[4]

The dining room is separated from the living room by the groin-vaulted reception hall, which "encourages a welcome feeling of progress

from one thing to another," Patterson noted. "It is an attractive idea and one which should be appreciated by women who like to trail their silks and chiffons effectively through long corridors."[5] In contrast with the interior's dominant English theme, the dining room is inspired by the Italian tradition. Its tiled floor and tinted bottle glass windows cool the room, while the coffered ceiling and carved window surrounds add a sculptural dimension. The magnificent pecky cypress ceiling in the eastern wing's second-story master bedroom was added in recent years, but the antique fireplace ornament is original to the room. The master bedroom also has a small balcony facing the ocean and deep porches off the his-and-her bathrooms.

Fatio incorporated passive (and timeless) methods of temperature control throughout, orienting the house to take advantage of prevailing eastern breezes and including at least two exposures in all major rooms. To the same end he also used up-to-the-minute technology, including motor-operated bronze sash windows in the pool room, which open

onto an outdoor swimming pool. The windows disappear into the floor, completely blurring the relationship between interior and exterior, a goal extolled by avant-garde architects of European modernism.[6] Fatio also included automated awnings to protect sunbathers.

Casa della Porta, one of Palm Beach's finest residences, has been subject to several careful restorations. In 1993 the Preservation Foundation of Palm Beach honored it with a Ballinger Award for outstanding historic restoration.[7] Subsequently the entrance figures and other carvings, leaded glass windows, and groin-vaulted ceiling were restored, and parasitic vegetation removed from the coquina walls—all painstakingly recapturing the exceptional quality of the original design.

1. Emilie C. Keyes, "McAneeny Home, Marvel of Charm is New Palm Beach Show Place," January 13, 1929, Archives of the Historical Society of Palm Beach County.

2. Augusta Owen Patterson, "A Palm Beach House in Native Stone," *Town and Country* 15 (December 1929).

3. "W. J. McAneeny, 62, Auto Official, Dies," *New York Times*, March 25, 1935, 16.

4. Patterson, 3.

5. Ibid.

6. Fatio's fellow Swiss architect Le Corbusier was a member of the European avant-garde. Fatio expressed an interest in "the modern movement in architecture and furniture" and sought out Le Corbusier's work. Letter from Fatio, October 10, 1927, in Alexandra Fatio, comp. and ed., *Maurice Fatio Architect* (Stuart, Florida: Southeastern Printing, 1992), 58–59.

7. Polly Anne Earl, *Palm Beach: An Architectural Legacy* (New York: Rizzoli; and Palm Beach: Preservation Foundation of Palm Beach, 2002), 2.

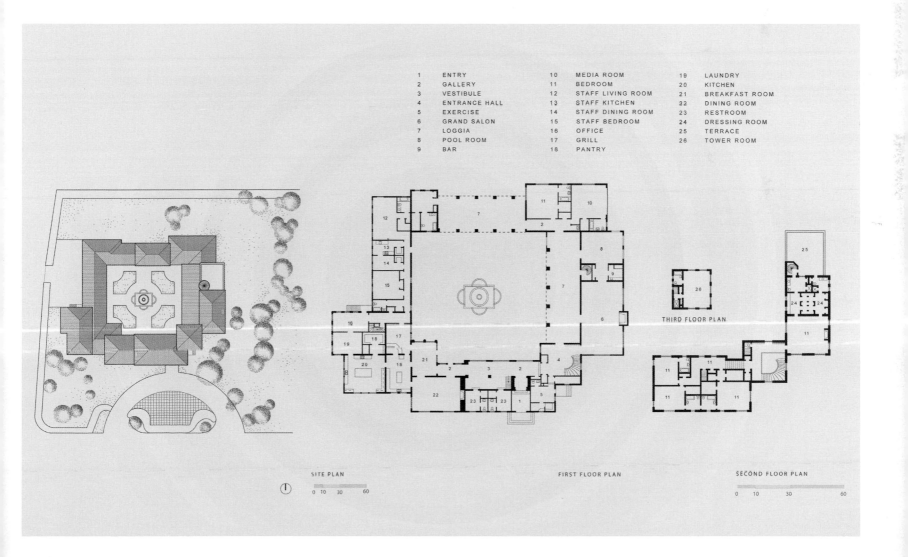

| 1 | ENTRY | 10 | MEDIA ROOM | 19 | LAUNDRY |
|---|---|---|---|---|---|
| 2 | GALLERY | 11 | BEDROOM | 20 | KITCHEN |
| 3 | VESTIBULE | 12 | STAFF LIVING ROOM | 21 | BREAKFAST ROOM |
| 4 | ENTRANCE HALL | 13 | STAFF KITCHEN | 22 | DINING ROOM |
| 5 | EXERCISE | 14 | STAFF DINING ROOM | 23 | RESTROOM |
| 6 | GRAND SALON | 15 | STAFF BEDROOM | 24 | DRESSING ROOM |
| 7 | LOGGIA | 16 | OFFICE | 25 | TERRACE |
| 8 | POOL ROOM | 17 | GRILL | 26 | TOWER ROOM |
| 9 | BAR | 18 | PANTRY | | |

SITE PLAN

0  10  30  60

FIRST FLOOR PLAN

THIRD FLOOR PLAN

SECOND FLOOR PLAN

0  10  30  60

# TRE FONTANE

*Marion Sims Wyeth*

*House*

Above: Garden. Opposite: Entrance

## MARION SIMS WYETH WAS AMONG PALM BEACH'S PRIME DESIGNERS.

His residential works ranged from modest houses to palatial estates like Mar-a-Lago, built in collaboration with Joseph Urban for Marjorie Merriweather Post and now owned by Donald Trump. Altogether, his work helped establish the city's graceful Mediterranean character. In 1924 he designed a house there for himself and his family, Tre Fontane.

Wyeth had arrived in Palm Beach in 1919, after four years at the École des Beaux-Arts in Paris, a year in Rome, and stints in the architectural firms of Bertram Grosvenor Goodhue and Carrère and Hastings (which had designed the Mediterranean-style Hotel Ponce de León in Saint Augustine, Florida, in 1885). Wyeth shared a New York office with Frederic Rhinelander King, with whom he created the firm Wyeth and King.[1]

Tre Fontane was built in a quiet neighborhood near the commercial center, one of the first houses in a new subdivision platted by developer Paris Singer, Addison Mizner's onetime collaborator. As the houses did not face water, their designs tended to be focused inward on a central courtyard and the surrounding landscape. Originally this was the case for Tre Fontane, but the subsequent acquisition of an adjacent parcel provided direct access to the beach.

Wyeth's characteristic architectural restraint is evident at Tre Fontane, whose entrance facade is simple to the point of severity; the virtually blank wall is broken by only a central arched opening surmounted by a stone cartouche. Drawing upon his classical education and knowledge of Italian Mediterranean houses, he skillfully integrated two organizing principles: the axis

Above: Loggia. Opposite: Dining room

and the courtyard. A strict east-west axis runs from the entrance to a courtyard fountain and continues through the loggia and two pairs of French doors to a wall fountain in the garden beyond. Originally there were three fountains along this axis (one for each of Wyeth's daughters, and the source of the house's name), but the loggia fountain was removed. The central open-air courtyard, surrounded by a colonnaded "cloister," is the house's focal point, providing access to the major public spaces, service wing, and second floor via an outdoor staircase. The courtyard's dimensions echo those of the loggia. The second floor integrates well with the courtyard, with a gallery that looks down on its eastern cloister and links the family's and servants' bedrooms.

Wyeth used distinct decorative schemes for different rooms, possibly using his home as a showcase that would demonstrate his range to prospective clients. The dining room has a rustic character, with a cross-beamed ceiling, simple white walls, and Cuban tile floor. The sense of space was later extended by a deep canopy in the garden. The loggia's ceiling, supported by groin vaults and corbels, gives the illusion of being vaulted. The loggia has historically been furnished with wicker, emphasizing its quasi-outdoor character. The living room presents the most formal appearance, with its elaborately painted wood ceiling and carved fireplace surround. The furniture is luxuriously upholstered, and window seats enhance the warm, comfortable atmosphere.

Opposite: Garden fountain. Above: View of courtyard

Careful changes to the exterior include the 1980 addition of a garage and the conversion of the existing garage (whose integration into the house plan was innovative in 1924) into living space. A pool, a two-story pool house/guest quarters, and a colonnaded pavilion linking the pool with the garden were other additions. Lush tropical planting surrounds the house, and the current owners have reinstated native plant material on the sand-covered parcel facing the ocean.

Tre Fontane reflects Wyeth's financial success and social status in Palm Beach, as well as the attention to detail he brought to all his work, whether he was designing a grand villa or a more modest family home.

1. Description of the Marion Sims Wyeth Architectural Collection, Preservation Foundation of Palm Beach, www.palmbeachpreservation.org, August 20, 2007.

Above: Living room. Below: Bathroom. Opposite: Pool view

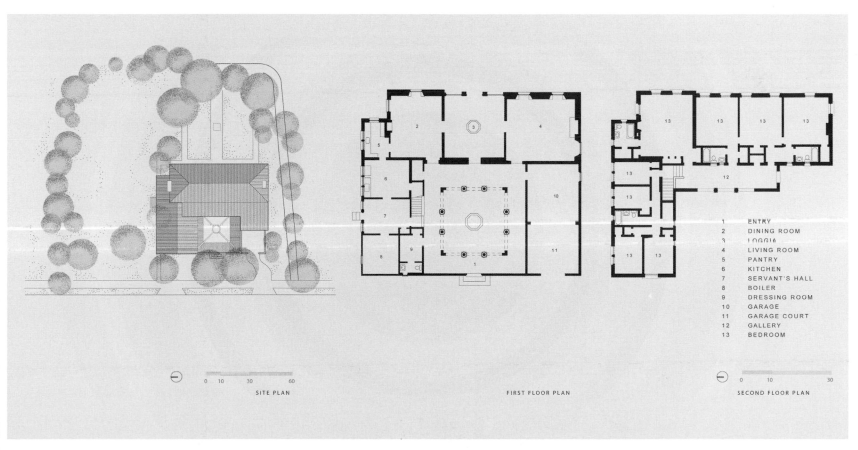

| | |
|---|---|
| 1 | ENTRY |
| 2 | DINING ROOM |
| 3 | LOGGIA |
| 4 | LIVING ROOM |
| 5 | PANTRY |
| 6 | KITCHEN |
| 7 | SERVANT'S HALL |
| 8 | BOILER |
| 9 | DRESSING ROOM |
| 10 | GARAGE |
| 11 | GARAGE COURT |
| 12 | GALLERY |
| 13 | BEDROOM |

SITE PLAN

FIRST FLOOR PLAN

SECOND FLOOR PLAN

# Pinewood

❦

*Charles Austin Buck*

*House*

Above: Dining room. Opposite: Moongate garden

## ARCHITECTURE USUALLY GUIDES A PROPERTY'S DESIGN, WITH LANDSCAPE

providing a backdrop. But Pinewood, the house and garden of Charles Austin Buck in Lake Wales, Florida, began with the landscape, which dictated the overall design. Pinewood was conceived by William Lyman Phillips, a landscape architect, and Charles R. Wait, an architect deeply familiar with landscape architecture's principles.

The client, a Pennsylvania native, was a director of Bethlehem Steel Corporation and president of several of its subsidiaries.[1] His wife had met an untimely death in 1925, leaving him with nine children. Shortly thereafter Buck visited his sister and brother-in-law in Mountain Lake, a planned residential community in Lake Wales designed by the nation's leading landscape architects, Olmsted Brothers.[2] In 1930 he purchased the 7.59 acres adjacent to his sister's property. Pinewood was completed two years later.

Mountain Lake was the brainchild of Frederick Ruth, a Maryland native whose family had begun acquiring the land in the late nineteenth century. Ruth wanted to develop it along the lines of Roland Park, a residential community Olmsted Brothers had laid out in the Baltimore suburbs, where architectural consistency was maintained by a design review committee. Ruth envisioned a winter resort where the elite "could enjoy a month or two with their families away from the stress of their occupations, yet in the company of others of great ability and accomplishment."[3]

Olmsted Brothers planned Mountain Lake in 1914–18. Two thousand acres were set aside for citrus groves and five hundred acres were designated for development with a country club, golf course, hotel, and winter homes along the shoreline of Moun-

Entrance hall

tain Lake. The landscaping and initial houses were designed by William Lyman Phillips, who was in charge of the local Olmsted office. Charles Wait—Olmsted's in-house architect until 1920—described the architectural vocabulary as "an infusion of [motifs] found in many of the Latin Countries where temperatures are mild. Such countries as Italy, Spain, the Caribbean and Bermuda. Let's call it Florida Spanish."[4]

Buck, who had worked in Cuba, Chile, and Venezuela, also favored a Mediterranean style for his house, which he called "El Retiro" (The Retreat),[5] and hired Phillips to determine the layout. The property, with native longleaf and cypress pines in abundance, is on the northwest slope of Iron Mountain, at a fairly high elevation by Florida standards: from 290 feet above sea level at the southeast corner to 255 feet at the northwest corner. Phillips recommended the house be oriented toward distant views along the long western axis and toward near views to the east. He wanted to capture southerly views by extending a wing to the northwest and "reconcile the obliquity of the house to the boundaries of the upper part of the lot by means of more or less formal areas of irregular shape."[6] He also suggested an informal lawn framed by native and exotic plants, including palm trees, a pond near the property's western corner, and a wild garden along the southern property line that would not "express any definite boundary." This portion of the property abuts the Bok Sanctuary, the Mountain Lakes preserve whose carillon, Bok Tower, is a historic landmark.

In the upper part of the lot, east of the house, Phillips proposed grading the surface to enlarge the forecourt, constructing retaining walls to further define the space, and building a grotto to accentuate the "effect of thrusting into the hillside."[7] The elaboration of the eastern portion of the property, which eventually included a small citrus grove near the grotto and a "frog fountain" from Cuba at the lower level, addressed Phillips's concern that the house had no obvious entry point. Other features that effectively created outdoor rooms were a sunny terrace (now shaded by mature trees) and, beyond the northwest wing, the Moongate Garden. The latter had a Chinese gate motif at the end of rectangular lawn bordered by a hedge and flowers; it was completed almost precisely as Phillips had envisioned it.

Bathroom

*The gate screen, in China, is used to keep out evil spirits, who can only travel in a straight line, so that a simple detour is enough to keep them out. Aside from this very practical advantage the arrangement is interesting aesthetically since it makes a composition with a great deal more relief and play of light and shade than would be possible with a simple panel on the wall. The decoration of the gate screen could be done with colored tiles—I can get some quite good Mexican ones in Tampa. . . . We could have a colored light . . . which ought to give an exotic effect, looking out from the dining room in the evening.*[8]

In accordance with Phillips's site plan, Charles Wait (who by this time had established a practice with Ernst May Parsons[9]) designed the twelve-thousand-square-foot house in a sprawling Y-shaped configuration similar to that of the California ranch house, then emerging as a residential type. Wait made creative use of the shifts in grade: From the entrance hall (at the junction of the main portion of the house and its northeast wing), stairs lead down to the public rooms on the first floor or up to the bedrooms on the second floor. To capture breezes, screened porches project from the east and west sides near the southern end, as well as from the dining room, with views of the Moongate Garden.

The interior has an informal quality. Exquisite tile Buck purchased in Cuba covers the floors, stair risers, and the dado lining the descending staircase, dining room, and powder room. A loggia on the first floor has large, arched pocket doors opening to the east and west. The adjacent living room is divided into a one-and-a-half-story space—which, with its tall gabled ceiling and wide doors to the porches, has an open character—and a contrastingly intimate alcove. The dining room has a large carved fireplace and a jewel-like quality owing to its extensive use of Cuban tile. Throughout, the walls were sheathed in unpainted white gypsum plaster (over hollow-tile construction). All exposed woodwork, including box beams and joists in the ceilings of the public rooms, is stained with a black oil resin.[10]

The exterior's rusticity is consistent with Buck's desire for an informal family retreat. The long body of the house is articulated by projecting elements, including the entrance and morning room bay, a circular stair tower, the porches, and the dining room extension, which break up the house's mass. The most ornamental details are the scored ashlar surrounds of the loggia doors, the pairs of columns supporting the screen porches, and a handsome row of garage doors. The walls are sheathed with integrally colored pink stucco—pale enough to appear bleached by the sun. The effects of weather and time are simulated by a terra-cotta-colored cement wash applied to the window and door details.

Pinewood's architectural deference to its landscape resulted in a felicitous balance of interior and exterior. The significance of this singular interpretation of the Mediterranean Revival was recognized by a listing in the National Register of Historic Places.

1. Schwarz, 3.

2. Documentation of the Olmsted project is housed in the Frederick Law Olmsted National Historic Site, Brookline, Mass., with a brief summary available at the Olmsted Research Guide, www.rediscov.com/olmsted, August 20, 2007.

3. John W. Caldwell, *Mountain Lake: A History* (Lake Wales, Fla.: Mountain Lake Corp., 1984), 9, quoted in Schwarz, 14.

4. Letter from Charles R. Wait to Thomas D. Ruth, June 27, 1968, quoted in Schwarz, 16.

5. Schwarz, 1. Subsequent owners changed the name. Ruth G. Keen, who bought the property in 1952, called it Keenwood. The American Foundation (now the Bok Tower Gardens Foundation), which acquired it in 1970, renamed it Pinewood for the longleaf and cypress pines "which are the dominant and most impressive feature of the landscape." Letter from Kenneth D. Morrison to Mr. and Mrs. D. Wood Keen, December 11, 1970, quoted in Schwarz, 10.

6. Schwarz, 30.

7. Ibid., 42.

8. Ibid., 48.

9. Ibid., 24.

10. Ibid., 54.

Opposite left: Living room, looking to alcove. Opposite right: Pinewood estate, view of Bok Tower. Above: Loggia (library)

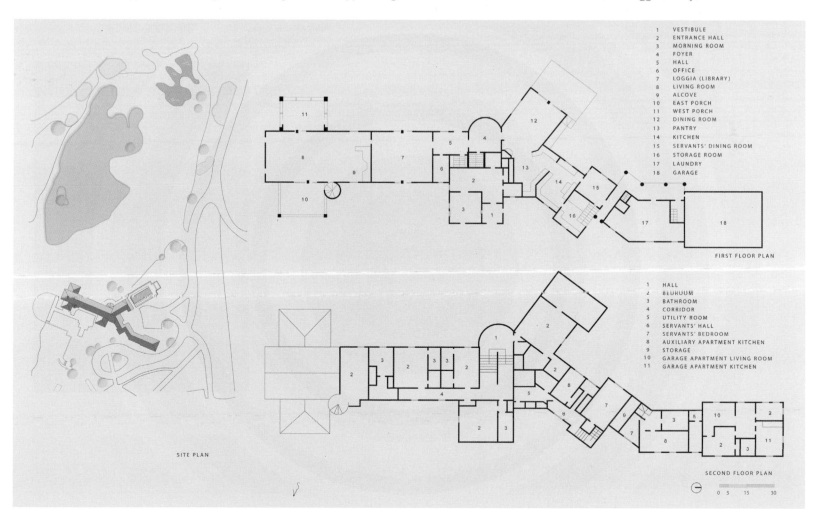

| | |
|---|---|
| 1 | VESTIBULE |
| 2 | ENTRANCE HALL |
| 3 | MORNING ROOM |
| 4 | FOYER |
| 5 | HALL |
| 6 | OFFICE |
| 7 | LOGGIA (LIBRARY) |
| 8 | LIVING ROOM |
| 9 | ALCOVE |
| 10 | EAST PORCH |
| 11 | WEST PORCH |
| 12 | DINING ROOM |
| 13 | PANTRY |
| 14 | KITCHEN |
| 15 | SERVANTS' DINING ROOM |
| 16 | STORAGE ROOM |
| 17 | LAUNDRY |
| 18 | GARAGE |

FIRST FLOOR PLAN

| | |
|---|---|
| 1 | HALL |
| 2 | BEDROOM |
| 3 | BATHROOM |
| 4 | CORRIDOR |
| 5 | UTILITY ROOM |
| 6 | SERVANTS' HALL |
| 7 | SERVANTS' BEDROOM |
| 8 | AUXILIARY APARTMENT KITCHEN |
| 9 | STORAGE |
| 10 | GARAGE APARTMENT LIVING ROOM |
| 11 | GARAGE APARTMENT KITCHEN |

SITE PLAN

SECOND FLOOR PLAN

0  5    15        30

# ROBERTA COKE
## *and*
# ALEX C. CAMP
# HOUSE

Above: Morning room. Opposite: Balcony

ONE OF TEXAS'S MOST IMPORTANT EXAMPLES OF ARCHITECTURAL regionalism is the Roberta Coke and Alex C. Camp house, which represents a pivotal step between traditional style and modernism. It was designed by John F. Staub, among the state's leading architects of the 1930s and 1940s and a proponent of regionalism, an architectural movement that documented local, historic, vernacular buildings, then borrowed and distilled their features in new works.

The house was built in 1936–38 on twenty-two wooded acres near the shore of Dallas's White Rock Lake. The landscape has since been remade into groomed botanical gardens. In the 1970s the Dallas Arboretum and Botanical Society purchased the estate, rehabilitating the house for receptions and its own offices. The arboretum also encompasses Rancho Encinal, Everett Lee and Nell Goodrich DeGolyer's property, designed after a Mexican hacienda by Beverly Hills architects Burton A. Scott and H. Denman Schutt in 1940.

In the Camp house, Staub referred to a number of local traditions, including the popular Mediterranean style, but simplified them almost to the point of abstraction. The U-configured floor plan is characteristically Mediterranean—indeed, it is reminiscent of a more traditional house Staub designed for Mr. and Mrs. William J. Crabb in Houston in 1935. Considered Staub's only Spanish house, the Crabb residence (since demolished) wrapped in a U around a central loggia, with stepped-back volumes on one end and a large two-story block on the other.[1]

Just a few years later, Staub pushed that traditional design in a modern direction at the Camp house by paring down and isolating each exterior component. He divided the south-facing entrance facade into discrete, unornamented cubic volumes:

Above: Living room. Opposite: Dining room

From west to east, there's a two-story wing with a balcony, a simply articulated two-story block with a gable end, a deeply recessed entrance porch, then a tall, battered chimney attached to a one-story volume that wraps around the east side. The enormous chimney functions as a stand-alone sculpture, underscoring the distinction of each of the balanced but asymmetrical volumes that together comprise the house.

Drawing again on local Mediterranean and adobe traditions, Staub emphasized the outdoors with a large terrace accessible from the entrance hall, library, living room, morning room, and guest room, which are arranged one room deep in a stepped plan. Another terrace extends the dining area, and a balcony and sun deck open up the second floor. The house is oriented toward the northwest, taking advantage of prevailing southern breezes. A number of the rooms have three to four exposures, and most windows run from floor to ceiling and slide into head or side pockets, further increasing air flow.

The design also springs from other local traditions. Stephen Fox, author of a 2007 book on Staub, suggested that the low-pitched gable roof evokes the vernacular houses of Castroville, a town just west of San Antonio settled by Alsatians in the 1840s. The houses there were typically whitewashed masonry structures with metal-sheathed gable roofs; Staub similarly built the Camp house of white-painted brick with a terne metal roof. Staub also incorporated what he called the Latin Colonial—a reference to the influence of New Orleans on the Gulf Coast of Texas—in the second-story balcony with wrought-iron detailing that wraps the house's southwest corner and is accessed by an exterior stair.

In all, the house presents an abstract exploration of locally familiar domestic devices. The gable, for example, is unornamented, very shallow, and visually supported by unornamented, shallow piers that integrate the gable into that section's mass. Staub thus referred to

architectural traditions while commenting on their structural irrelevance, translating the local architectural vocabulary into the language of modern design.

In a 1942 article on Staub, James Chillman Jr., who was the first director of the Museum of Fine Arts, Houston, and a professor of art history at Rice University, discussed the Camp house's "expressiveness of the culture which produces it. . . . Each house is more than a soundly-built shelter; it is a home, and each is a clear interpretation of the ideals of the South, not of tradition, but of today."[2]

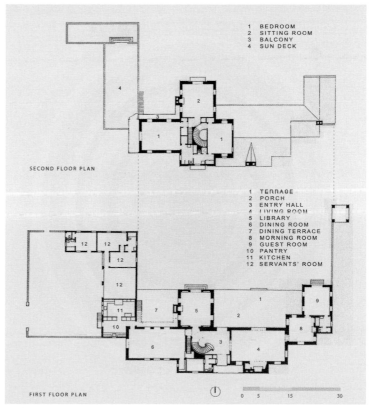

1. Howard Barnstone, *The Architecture of John F. Staub: Houston and the South* (Austin: Published in cooperation with the Museum of Fine Arts, Houston [by] University of Texas Press, c. 1979) 195–97.

2. Chillman, 22.

# MARSHALL *and* PATRICIA STEVES HOUSE

Above: Street view. Opposite: Gallery

WHILE OTHER TEXAS CITIES RELINQUISHED MUCH OF THEIR VINTAGE

architecture in the name of modernism after World War II, San Antonio preserved a sense of its past, and much of its new construction has been designed to complement the city's historic character. The Marshall and Patricia Steves residence (1964–65) exemplifies the modern house that maintains a connection with the past. *House & Garden* magazine, which named it Hallmark House of 1967, described it as "contemporary in the way it works and is lived in without conforming at all to the starker aspects of modern design."[1]

The Steveses worked closely with the architectural firm Ford, Powell & Carson on the design. O'Neil Ford, a well-known Texas architect, had designed a house for Marshall's brother and knew the Steveses as fellow members of the San Antonio Conservation Society, a nonprofit preservation and land conservation group.[2] Ford's young associate Chris Carson—known within the firm for his "unerring ability to make the right choices"[3]—took on the Steves project.

The Steveses wanted a modern house that referenced San Antonio's Latin past, nearby Mexico, and more distant Spanish traditions. Their fourteen-thousand-square-foot house was sited on two-and-a-half suburban acres. The design was inspired by the inward-looking hacienda. A virtually solid entrance facade and encircling garden wall created privacy, allowing interiors to stretch into the outdoors in a relaxed fashion. Ford saw the sequestered house as both a contemporary response to the need for private spaces in the face of population growth and a more general reference to San Antonio's heritage: "Had San Antonio

remained a Spanish town and grown into something other than a frontier outpost and site of the missions, I am sure that city houses with walled gardens would have been built everywhere."[4]

Notwithstanding the historic references, the plan is thoroughly modern: essentially a linear spine off which rooms and courtyards extend, like a "flagpole with flags coming off it."[5] It derived from the binuclear plan, which specified separate wings for public and private rooms, developed by the German modernist architect Marcel Breuer. Ford previously had employed it, including at the 1954 Evons house in San Antonio, which the Steveses had visited. Often configured as an H or a U, the binuclear plan spatially organized domestic life, separating the zones of the house with courtyards.[6] In the context of the Southwest, the binuclear house brought together a modern, functional plan and the traditional Latin use of patios and terraces as extensions of the living space.

At the Steves house, the fountain patio separates the bedrooms from the entrance and public spaces; the Santiago patio is between the living room and large game room; and the pool patio lies across from the game room. The centerpiece is the hundred-foot-long, nineteen-foot-high gallery. Its imposing vertical orientation is balanced by the abundant light flowing into it from patios projecting to the north and south. It is a soft light that reflects off the thick stuccoed walls around the patios. Additional warmth and visual interest come from a series of nine brick vaults or *bovedas* that are illuminated by small cupolas. Another *boveda* surmounts the dining room.

The Steveses and Ford first saw *bovedas* when they traveled to Mexico at the start of the project to research vernacular architecture. There the group met Giorgio Belloli, an architect and collector, whose brick-domed house was constructed according to an ancient method practiced by a handful of masons known as *bovederos*. The *boveda* is a type of masonry vault constructed without benefit of temporary shoring supports or centering. Special lightweight bricks called *ladrillos*— eight inches long, four inches wide, and two inches thick—are laid with sticky high-slump mortar. A master *bovedero* from Jalisco, Mateo Avila of Lagos de Moreno, built the Steves house vaults. The *bovedas* are essential to the house's character, creating an authentic connection to an ancient Mexican and Mediterranean-derived construction method, and adding beautiful, organic shapes that dramatically contrast with the tall, white plaster walls.

Opposite: Game room. Above: Living room. Below: Bedroom

Opposite: Living room staircase. Above: Entrance

The Steveses also acquired architectural fragments in Mexico that were integrated into the design. The main entrance is an old monastery door from Guanajuato; Ford's brother Lynn added decorative lead panels to the interior side. An eighteenth-century stone arcade from Morella spans the fountain patio near the entrance, where an eighteenth-century baptismal font serves as the fountain. A circular stone staircase from Pueblo (c. 1760) leads to a loft library at the far end of the living room, and rooms throughout the house are adorned by antique fireplace mantels. Paving stones from Queretaro and tiles from Saltillo add to the sense of Mexican verisimilitude.

The Steves house was constructed as modernism was reaching its apex in American architecture, and it was unusual if not risky for an architect of O'Neil Ford's stature to be associated with such a "romantic and decorative home."[7] Yet Ford was extremely proud of it and brought visitors to see it until his death in 1982.[8] And architects continue to draw inspiration from the Steves house; members of the American Institute of Architects toured it in 2007 as part of the organization's sesquicentennial celebration. It exemplifies how incorporating authentic historical references within a modern, functional dwelling can define a sense of place in a thoroughly contemporary fashion.

1. "H&G's Hallmark House for 1967," *House & Garden* 131 (April 1967), 126.

2. Author's interview with Patricia Steves, March 6, 2007.

3. Mary Carolyn Hollers George, *O'Neil Ford, Architect* (College Station, Tex.: Texas A&M University Press, 1992), 162.

4. Letter from Ford to Marvin Eickenroht, January 15, 1965, quoted in George, 184.

5. Interview with Patricia Steves.

6. Antonio Armesto, "Fifteen American Houses by Marcel Breuer," 2G 17 (2001), 11–12.

7. George, 168.

8. Ibid., 184.

Opposite: Dining room. Above: Pool patio

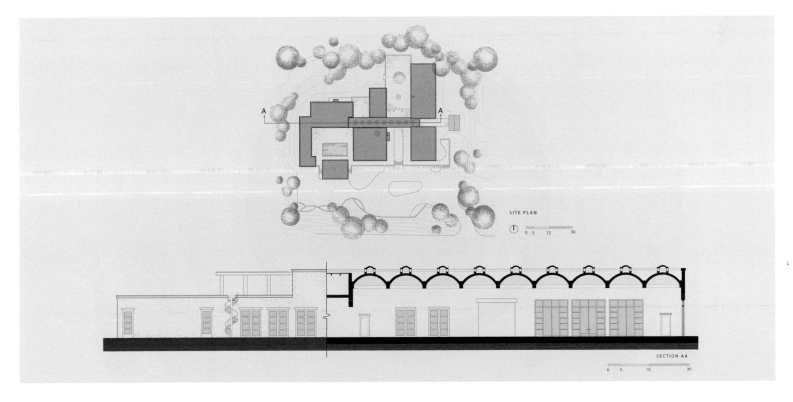

SITE PLAN

SECTION AA

# WINTER-SWEENEY HOUSE

# Most Mediterranean houses in the United States connect

to the Mediterranean tradition via Spain and Italy or their New World descendants. The Winter-Sweeney house (1981) in San Antonio, Texas, was inspired by an older source: Greece. Architect Chris Carson of Ford, Powell & Carson did not turn to ancient Greece's familiar classical architecture but instead drew upon the vernacular house that can still be found in small Greek villages, emulating its simplicity of form and direct response to climate and topography—qualities shared with other outstanding Mediterranean houses.

The project began with a trip to Greece, where Carson, who is of Greek descent, and Joan Brown Winter found they shared an interest in village houses and small churches. Winter asked Carson to develop a plan for a San Antonio residence based on the houses they had seen together.[1] Both believed a Greek villa would be suitable in San Antonio due to similarities of bright light and dry climate. On another trip they visited some of Greece's most important intact villages and small towns, including Makrynitsa, Volos, and the islands of Hydra and Spetses. They purchased architectural fragments dating to 1800–1910 from structures being torn down for new apartment buildings. These were incorporated into the design of the new house.

Making an analogy to a Greek village, Carson designed a one-story house—set atop a hill on a two-acre lot—that reads as a series of structures built over time around a central courtyard; there's an exterior staircase, an alleyway, and even what appears to be a church (actually a double-height library). Entry is through a gateway that pierces a virtually blank west facade. The garage roof serves as a terrace, with a pergola and a freestanding fireplace. A guesthouse and pool house complete the enclosure of buildings. Through

Opposite: Garden view. Above: Living room. Below: Bedroom

Above: Dining room. Opposite: Library

the east gate, the pool area is paved with limestone laid in a random pattern, a traditional Peloponnesian technique. The waters flow through a fragment of a stone aqueduct into the pool, which is surrounded by bougainvillea, plumbagos, and sago palms. The original landscape design was by James E. Keeter, who worked extensively with Joan Winter. The current owner, E. J. Sweeney, introduced Mediterranean plants that require little water and thrive in this setting as they do in Greece.

The materials used are common in Greek architecture: white limestone, travertine, marble, and terra-cotta (for the barrel-shaped roof tiles and ornaments), with stucco walls and exposed wood beams throughout. Doors and shuttered windows are painted a distinctive blue-green Carson discovered on Hydra; he brought a paint sample back with him. The drive is paved with large cobbled stones, and the inspiration for the distinctive and varied chimney caps (there are five fireplaces) came from trips to Greek islands. Other sculptural details, such as the acroteria, terra-cotta elements along the roof line, add to the authenticity that permeates the house. A large Aleppo pine native

to the Mediterranean anchors the center of the courtyard, which is planted with olive and fig trees, oleanders, cypress, and rosemary.

The exterior's white simplicity carries into the main house and becomes part of its clean, modern geometry. Built one room deep, the house is carefully oriented in relation to San Antonio's intense sunlight and prevailing southeast breezes. The floors of the entrance hall, living room, and dining room are laid with large random pieces of travertine marble, corresponding to the adjacent serpentine terrace, which is laid with random limestone pieces. An exception to the house's overall horizontal flow is the library, with its emphatic verticality. A dark-stained exposed truss spans the tall space; incised beneath it is a Greek aphorism that translates as "Knowledge is the source and Greece is the river." Suspended from one beam is a brass chandelier that could have come from a Byzantine church. Ecclesiastical incense burners were adapted as pendant lights for the barrel-vaulted hallway, which features a kore (standing female figure) at one end; a Hellenistic balustrade of Pentelic marble carved in the shape of a griffin is embedded in a dining room wall.

As he did at the Steves house, Chris Carson integrated a vernacular architectural tradition with a thoroughly modern house plan for Winter-Sweeney and incorporated historic architectural fragments to link past and present. However, the Winter-Sweeney house, designed about sixteen years later, retains the geometric simplicity associated with modern design.[2] The unique ingredient he added was the homage to the Greek contribution to the Mediterranean house.

1. Author's interview with Chris Carson, January 26, 2007, and e-mail correspondence, July 22, 2007.

2. This blend of modernism and sensitivity to local climate and culture reflected the contemporary Critical Regionalism movement. See Alex Tzonis and Liane Lefaivre, "The Grid and the Pathway: An Introduction to the Work of Dimitris and Susana Antonakakis," *Architecture in Greece* 15 (1981), 164–78.

Opposite: Terrace. Above: Library and hall

# ROSALIE *and* RICHARD ALTER HOUSE

Above: Pool view. Opposite: View from entrance into forecourt. Overleaf: Porch, looking toward the bay

# MEDITERRANEAN ARCHITECTURE TOOK ROOT IN SOUTHERN FLORIDA

in the early years of the twentieth century, drawing upon Spanish precedents adapted to a hot, humid climate by generations of architects in Spain's former Caribbean colonies, particularly Cuba. Though the style's popularity never waned in South Florida, it has been reinvigorated in recent decades by the energy, creativity, and Latin flavor brought by the influx of Cuban immigrants that began in the early 1960s.

One of the leading contributors to a new vision of the traditional Mediterranean house in South Florida is Havana-born architect Jorge Hernandez, who moved to Miami as a boy in 1962. At the Rosalie and Richard Alter house in Miami Beach, completed in 2004, Hernandez began with aspects of traditional design—including an enclosed courtyard, an arcade surmounted by a bank of windows, simple cornice and sill detailing, a columned circular terrace, and a richly carved antique Indian door at the street facade—but produced a distinctly contemporary result.

The house was designed as a winter residence for a couple that travels frequently between homes outside Baltimore and in Israel. It was built on a narrow, deep lot, formerly the site of a tennis court, with unobstructed views of Biscayne Bay. Hernandez oriented the house in a southern direction, toward the bay, both to maximize the narrow space and to provide privacy and protection on the street side. Making the most of the outdoor area, he based the floor plan on the traditional two-story side-yard plan associated with Charleston, South Carolina, where the house is set sideways to the street and deep in the lot, and the landscape is located to one side.[1]

Above: Living room. Below: Round porch. Opposite: Exterior staircase

The house gradually unfolds from the street, with an increasing sense of openness as it nears the bay: from a solid entrance facade to the enclosure of a large forecourt, through a triple-arched entry into the airy living/dining area, then to a deep porch that extends the living room outdoors. The rooms along this north-south axis suggest the dissolution of solid walls into space: Large windows at the northern end yield to French doors, which give way to wide openings to porches, until the architecture seems to melt into the outdoors before the bay. Two steps lead from the living room porch to the grassy terrace and pool, with the glinting waters of the Biscayne stretching beyond.

Hernandez has created a thoroughly comfortable, informal house at this sun-drenched waterfront location. Each room has a beautiful view, and several directly access a rooftop terrace. The French doors and large windows provide ample air circulation. Beyond such practi-

cal considerations, Hernandez created a dreamlike environment here, with both the rectangular abstraction formed by the lawn and pool and the array of whimsical elements: the virtually circular terrace whose roof is supported by large Tuscan columns of coquina stone (limestone); the curving, sculptural details of walls around the interior and exterior staircases; and the exterior staircase itself, which simply dead-ends just below the second story. Reminiscent of the paintings of Giorgio de Chirico, these architectural and landscape features appear almost detached from the forces of nature, lending the Alter house a timeless, almost surreal quality.

1. Hernandez had explored the side-yard plan in earlier schemes. See "Side-Yard House, Windsor (1992), collaborative project with Dennis Hector, Joanna Lombard, Francis Lyn," in Vincent Scully, *Between Two Towers* (New York: Monacelli Press, 1996), plate 96.

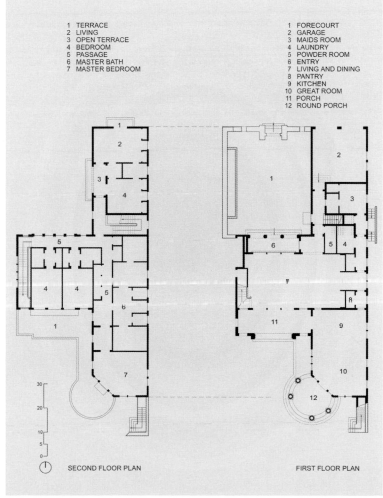

| 1 TERRACE | 1 FORECOURT |
| 2 LIVING | 2 GARAGE |
| 3 OPEN TERRACE | 3 MAIDS ROOM |
| 4 BEDROOM | 4 LAUNDRY |
| 5 PASSAGE | 5 POWDER ROOM |
| 6 MASTER BATH | 6 ENTRY |
| 7 MASTER BEDROOM | 7 LIVING AND DINING |
| | 8 PANTRY |
| | 9 KITCHEN |
| | 10 GREAT ROOM |
| | 11 PORCH |
| | 12 ROUND PORCH |

SECOND FLOOR PLAN      FIRST FLOOR PLAN

# Buzz Yudell
## *and* Tina Beebe
# House

Above: Rear view. Opposite: Living room

ONE OF THE MOST INTRIGUING MODERN INTERPRETATIONS OF A

Mediterranean house is the one architect Buzz Yudell and his wife, Tina Beebe—a graphic designer, landscape designer, and colorist—designed for themselves in Malibu, California, in 1989. Yudell studied architecture at Yale University with Charles W. Moore and Kent C. Bloomer; Beebe studied graphic design at Yale. Both worked with Moore in his Connecticut office, and Yudell later became a partner in the Los Angeles firm of Moore Ruble Yudell (MRY). Beebe is MRY's in-house specialist on color and materials; one of her early projects was to repaint the house Moore designed in 1973 for Lee Burns in Los Angeles (see fig. 22 in Introduction).

Their own house has a self-effacing quality that lets the dramatic landscape dominate; Yudell described his approach as "serene" and "restrained."[1] He designed a minimalist enclosure with numerous openings from room to room and to the outdoors; the overall effect is a natural flow of movement within the house and between the interior and exterior. A gallery broad enough for seating and dining links the rooms and provides access to the outdoors, much as a Mediterranean loggia does. Parallel to the gallery is a walkway, framed on the west by pergolas defining roofless outdoor rooms, which culminates at the south end in the pool court.

The two-story house (plus a tower) steps down a challenging site: a narrow lot—one hundred feet by six hundred feet—with a series of restrictions that effectively reduced the width of the buildable area to thirty-two feet. Moreover, the north-south axis slopes at a seven percent grade from the foothills of the Santa Monica Mountains toward the Pacific Ocean, and the west end drops into a dry creek bed covered with chaparral.

Above: Entry court. Below: Studio/guesthouse. Opposite: Studio/guesthouse

The site conditions dictated the house's vertical orientation, which also captures views of the ocean and the mountains. Yudell said, "We chose strong, simple shapes that fit into the landscape."[2] The exterior walls are covered in stucco; the roof is sheathed with standing-seam metal. With its simplicity and verticality—signatures of MRY's work—it is reminiscent of farmhouses in coastal California.

The ground floor seems to expand gradually from the entrance, at the north end, to the kitchen/dining and living rooms, at the south. This expansive quality results from an increasing penetration of solid walls by windows that allows light to suffuse the interior. A lustrousness arises from the Vicenza limestone flooring and the hint of warm color Beebe mixed directly into the plaster as it was troweled onto the walls. A double fireplace flanked by a pair of staircases separates the kitchen/dining area from the living room. On the second floor a double-height library leads on one side to the master bedroom and its sleeping porch, which affords views of the ocean, and on the other to the study and tower, with views toward the mountains.

Beebe, who comes from a long line of talented gardeners, designed the landscape, softening the retaining walls with plantings and creating a flow through cultivated gardens: an olive grove, a rose garden, a citrus grove, and planting beds with flowers and vegetables (sometimes

Above: Kitchen and dining area. Below: Master bedroom and sleeping porch. Opposite: Staircase

planted together). A parking court separates the main house from the two-story studio/guesthouse at the north end of the property.

In essence, Yudell and Beebe designed a modern house whose space, form, and landscape recall the Mediterranean. For Yudell, the Mediterranean tradition of enclosing the private realm within defensive outer walls seemed an apt solution to "our need to sense the security inside our dwelling place in order to act with strength in the outside community."[3] In 1991, when the house and garden were recognized with *Sunset* magazine's Western Home Award of Merit, a juror commented that they evoked "gentle memories of other places and other times, especially of Italian hill towns."[4]

1. Author's interview with Buzz Yudell and Tina Beebe, March 2, 2007.

2. Christine Pittel, "Earthly Delights," *House Beautiful* 134:8 (August 1992), 57.

3. Ibid.

4. "Mediterranean Roots, But Built for Today's Tight Lots," *Sunset*, October 1991, 95.

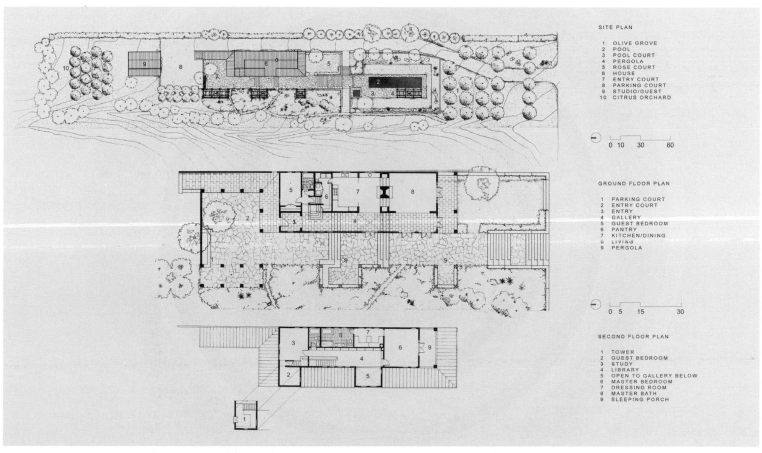

SITE PLAN

1  OLIVE GROVE
2  POOL
3  POOL COURT
4  PERGOLA
5  ROSE COURT
6  HOUSE
7  ENTRY COURT
8  PARKING COURT
9  STUDIO/GUEST
10  CITRUS ORCHARD

0  10    30      60

GROUND FLOOR PLAN

1  PARKING COURT
2  ENTRY COURT
3  ENTRY
4  GALLERY
5  GUEST BEDROOM
6  PANTRY
7  KITCHEN/DINING
8  LIVING
9  PERGOLA

0  5    15      30

SECOND FLOOR PLAN

1  TOWER
2  GUEST BEDROOM
3  STUDY
4  LIBRARY
5  OPEN TO GALLERY BELOW
6  MASTER BEDROOM
7  DRESSING ROOM
8  MASTER BATH
9  SLEEPING PORCH

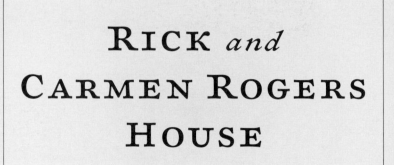

# RICK *and* CARMEN ROGERS HOUSE

❧

Above: Street view. Opposite: Dining room

## THE GREAT TRADITIONS OF THE MEDITERRANEAN HOUSE CLEARLY CAN BE

creatively employed in the twenty-first century without resulting in what architect Barton Myers referred to as the "terrible . . . Tuscans"[1]—as Myers's contemporary house for Rick and Carmen Rogers (2006) persuasively demonstrates. It was designed for a busy corner lot in a Westside Los Angeles neighborhood. Following the precedent of the walled Mediterranean urban house, Myers built it almost to the property lines to maximize the private outdoor space. From the street the house presents itself as a severe, minimalist composition, an effect that will be somewhat softened as vines grow up the entrance facade.

Past the defensive walls, the entry opens onto a large central courtyard with a mature Italian stone pine at its center. Adjacent to the courtyard's exterior wall is a lap pool of black-tinted concrete; it serves as a reflecting pool when not in use. Water spills continuously from the pool into an outer trough, and its gushing helps shield the courtyard from traffic noise during rush hour.[2] A massive steel sculpture by Texas artist Betty Gold hovers over the pool with seeming peril; it is anchored with large bolts into a concrete wall.

Flanking the courtyard are three buildings: a guesthouse, a garage and game room, and the main house, oriented to take full advantage of the southern exposure. The house is constructed of exposed industrial materials—a structural steel frame, a metal deck ceiling, and concrete floors—bathed in warm light from glazed openings on all four sides, which makes the roof appear to float. Glazed aluminum sectional doors lightly enclose the courtyard side. When the doors are open, the combined kitchen/living/dining room literally extends outdoors. Glass doors at the north end of the living area open onto an intimate rear garden;

another pair of glass doors to the south leads to an outdoor dining area. There's also a band of north-facing clerestory windows, offering views of the changing sky. Galvanized rolling shutters above every glazed opening serve as an envelope that provides security, insulation, and sun control.

A long corridor separates the public spaces from the media room, two bedrooms with baths, and a pantry near the kitchen. The master bedroom's large windows look onto the rear garden, giving the effect from inside of "being in a garden," according to Carmen Rogers.[3] Landscape architect Katherine Glascock planted a series of terraces with papyrus sprays, palms, bird of paradise, and other exotic plants. "There is so much glass in the house that we wanted something really good to look at out those windows," Rick Rogers said.[4]

The Rogerses selected Barton Myers as architect after seeing the house he built for himself on a hilly site in Montecito (1998) in *Sunset*

magazine, which had honored it with a Western Home Special Award. It embodied ideas they wanted in their own residence, including a large, open plan with the kitchen, dining room, and living room sharing one space. Myers's own house comprises four buildings on three terraces, sited to respect the topography and native landscape and to take advantage of views of the Channel Islands. Each building has an exposed structural steel frame with a metal deck ceiling, concrete retaining walls, concrete floors, and glazed aluminum sectional doors enclosing the southern exposure. Despite very different site conditions, the Rogerses could envision Myers's house adapted to their urban lot, essentially redeploying a terraced suburban villa as an urban courtyard palazzo.

The Rogers project continued Myers's decades-long fascination with steel construction, which he has used in residential design for its structural strength and the transparency it allows, resulting in a seamless relationship between interior and exterior space. That concept

Opposite: Kitchen. Above: Bedroom. Below: Living room

Barton Myers. Living room, Myers house, Montecito, California. 1998. The suburban house the architect built for himself inspired the Rogerses to commission him to design a house of similar components in a city setting.